For Christopher from
Gavin & Margo
with all our love
for 1978

Author's Dedication

£3·99

?

GW00726124

29th December 1977

New Poems 1977–78

THE P.E.N. ANTHOLOGIES
OF CONTEMPORARY POETRY

NEW POEMS

1977—78

A P.E.N. Anthology
of Contemporary Poetry

Edited by
GAVIN EWART

HUTCHINSON OF LONDON

Hutchinson & Co (Publishers) Ltd
3 Fitzroy Square, London W1

London Melbourne Sydney Auckland
Wellington Johannesburg and agencies
throughout the world

First published 1977
© Hutchinson & Co (Publishers) Ltd 1977

Set in Monotype Garamond
Printed in Great Britain by
The Anchor Press Ltd and bound by
Wm Brendon & Son Ltd, both of
Tiptree, Essex

ISBN 0 09 131790 8

ACKNOWLEDGEMENTS

Acknowledgements are due to the poets who have allowed their work to be reprinted or included here, and to the following publications in which the poems first appeared: *Akros, Ambit, Bananas, Cracked Lookingglass, Curtal Sails, Encounter, Fireweed, Gallery, Green Lines, Irish Press, London Magazine, Montage, New Poetry, Oasis, Outposts, Palantir, Pick, PN Review, POD, Poesis, PS, Quarto, Stony Thursday, Southern Review, Thames Poetry, The Honest Ulsterman, The Listener, The Little Word Machine, The New Review, The New Statesman, The Times Literary Supplement.* Also to New Poetry (BBC 3).

'Part of the Story', by Robert Vas Dias, appeared in *POD*, No. 1, copyright © 1976 by POD Books, edited by Kirby Malone (USA), and in *Green Lines*, No. 1, 1976, edited by Tim Dooley and Mark Helmore (London), and is reprinted with permission.

Permission to reprint or broadcast any poems in this anthology must be obtained from Hutchinson of London, 3 Fitzroy Square, London W1P 6JD, and the individual poet with whom the copyright rests. The usual acknowledgement must be made to the publishers and to *New Poems 1977–78*, the twentieth in the P.E.N. series of anthologies of contemporary poetry. Letters to contributors will be forwarded if addressed to International P.E.N. 62 Glebe Place, Chelsea, London SW3 5JB, England (telephone 01–352 9549 or 01–352 6303).

CONTENTS

INTRODUCTION

To compile an anthology is as hard to do (and do well) as to review one. All that is open to the reviewer, assuming that he accepts the need for a new anthology of Geriatric or Housewives' Verse, is to criticize the choice. There is far too much Armadillo. Why are Bison and Corncrake not represented?

Meeting such criticism is hard. Bison and Corncrake (poets of talent) might happen not to have written very good poems between April 1976 and April 1977 – or perhaps none at all. Or they might have been overlooked (quite possible). One function of this series of *New Poems* anthologies is to introduce new talent. To see the same old names all the time is not very exciting for the public; yet it must remain true that the poets of some reputation are the ones most likely to have written good new poems. Some good poems are going to be left out, some less good ones included – perhaps to exemplify a genre. An Editor can't read everything.

Concrete poetry and typewriter poetry are, because of the nature of the printing, excluded. So is sound poetry (which depends on live performance). Academic poetry, where culture and intelligence are deployed without very much 'human interest', is not represented. Nor is autotelic poetry – where the poem is an end in itself, with no desire to communicate, outstaring the reader with a blank 'Fuck you!' These kinds of poetry – in the interests of the general reader – have been excluded. Semantic poetry (in the Themerson sense) is also not represented, simply because there isn't any.

I have not tried, as previous Editors have, to group poems according to theme. This decision was not dictated by laziness but by the thought that, if authors appear in alphabetical order, they are a lot easier to find.

No one reader will enjoy everything printed here. My hope is that everything will be enjoyed by someone.

Gavin Ewart

Anna Adams

NATURE NOTE–APRIL 1975

Every year, at this season, in this same
waterfilled crease between tree-root and limestone,
motionless pickaback frog-gods proclaim—

> let there be frogspawn.

After an ice-age of unknown duration,
(frog-sleep was god-blink, a gap in time),
skygazing eyes make the world reassemble, and

> heavens resume their

contents – grey cloud and the habit of raining,
rook carbon-paper-chase through the bright morning,
fragmented arches of raucously homing

> birds in the evening:

great tides of darkness that glitter with sunspawn,
unspotted cumulus masses of windspawn
slowly dissolving. Meanwhile, in the frog-pool,

> many soft-glass domed

mansions with round rooms inhabited by
fullstops grown restless, unrolling to commas
eating their way towards writing life sentences,

> swell in the water.

Setting, each year, evolution in motion,
frog-gods' creative trance conjures man's embryo
form from the mud. Basic dances, repeated,

> pump the form fountain,

prove that beginning is always. Each god-blink
shatters us, makes us again. On time travels,
every Summer must reknit the link

> Winter unravels.

Not only meadows and swallows, for nothing's
made once and for all: time erodes terza-rima.
Wisdom forgets himself. Infants' first mouthings are

'Mama', not Homer.

Deborah Adams

AMELIA

Amelia's got one of those sweet
clean faces that looks
as if it's been scrubbed twice
before I've stumbled down to meet
her for breakfast.
We talked about mice

this morning, and somehow
Amelia can declare mice unnecessary
and they will disappear;
she once said, 'a cow
is ugly so why bother with
feeding it for milk, dear?'

The next day I looked high
and low but couldn't locate one
cow – that's her power of
the scrubbed rosy cheeks. I
think Amelia's some strange
being that belongs to 'them' above.

Fleur Adcock

THE INNER HARBOUR

Paua-Shell

Spilt petrol
oil on a puddle
the sea's colour-chart
porcelain, tie-dyed.
Tap the shell:
glazed calcium.

Cat's-Eye

Boss-eye, wall-eye, squinty lid
stony door for a sea-snail's tunnel

the long beach littered with them
domes of shell, discarded virginities

where the green girl wanders, willing
to lose hers to the right man

or to the wrong man, if he should raise
his frolic head above a sand-dune

glossy-black-haired, and that smile on him.

Sea-Lives

Under the sand at low tide
are whispers, hisses, long slithers,
bubbles, the suck of ingestion, a soft
snap: mysteries and exclusions.

Things grow on the dunes too –
pale straggle of lupin-bushes,

cutty-grass, evening primroses
puckering in the low light.

But the sea knows better.
Walk at the edge of its rich waves:
on the surface nothing shows;
underneath it is fat and fecund.

Shrimping-Net

Standing just under the boatshed
kneedeep in dappled water
sand-coloured legs and the sand itself
greenish in the lit ripples
watching the shrimps avoid her net
little flexible glass rockets
and the lifted mesh always empty
gauze and wire dripping sunlight

She is too tall to stand under
this house. It is a fantasy

And moving in from the bright outskirts
further under the shadowy floor
hearing a footstep creak above
her head brushing the rough timber
edging further bending her knees
creosote beams grazing her shoulder
the ground higher the roof lower
sand sifting on to her hair

She kneels in dark shallow water,
palms pressed upon shells and weed.

Kingsley Amis

A REUNION

Dear Bill, To confirm – we meet
At the Allied Services Club,
6 Upper Greenhill Street
(Opposite Farringdon Tube),
On Friday 11th July
Any time after 6 p.m.;
Informal – but wear a tie!
Yours very sincerely, Jim.

Thirty years ago
Jim had been Sergeant Woods,
The chap you did well to know
If you wanted some over-the-odds
Bit of kit, travel warrant, repair;
A lot came his way from his friend
The O.C., Major MacClure –
One of those who had 'hoped to attend'.

I hoped so too, on the whole,
As I started off: you could say
That Sandy MacClure was a real
Panjandrum of shits on his day,
But the bugger could get you to laugh:
Killing take-offs of his mates,
The booby-traps sprung on the Staff,
That truck-load of Yank cigarettes.

Jim was a quieter lad,
Ever willing to reminisce
About life in Hyderabad,
And also to take the piss;
A fine bloody pair they were
(My Christ, how they screwed around)
To remember so loud and clear,
But others soon came to mind:

Slosher Perkins, disciple of Marx,
With his pamphlets and posters; Burnett
(Was he one of the company clerks?),
The booziest sod of the lot;
Young Taylor, obstreperous enough
In spite of that choirboyish look;
Shy little Corporal Clough,
Who would talk about Shelley and Blake.

And behind them a hundred more
With a background of pay-parades,
The Naafi, the technical store,
Being lectured about grenades,
Guard-mounting, vehicle pools,
Defaulters, inspections of kit
And barrack-rooms, spares and tools,
And gas-capes and God knows what.

Then farmyards and cobbled roads
Full of sun, fresh fruit, village wells,
Tents pitched in the leaf-strewn woods,
Slow crossing of iced-up canals,
Those seasons, that mutable scene
Trodden through in the end – all that,
Plus litres of lager and wine
And a sniff or so at the frat.*

II
Now, up a green-linoed stair,
Past walls in need of a wash
I went, turned a corner, and there
Was Jim, with a grey moustache
And a belly, but still – 'Good God!'
I said, 'you look just the same,
You treacherous, miserable sod!'
'I'm sorry,' he said – 'what's the name?'

* 'Fraternization' between Allied troops and German nationals, including
females, was forbidden by order of General Eisenhower in 1944. Phrases
like 'a piece of frat' soon became current.

Soon seen to. The place had the look
Of a rather expensive canteen:
Sandwiches, cakes and cake,
Card-tables, a fruit-machine,
A fag-machine and a bar.
This served in effect, I found,
Scotch, gin and tonic, and beer;
You struggled to stand your round.

Oh, one other drink, ginger ale,
Stood before my incredulous eye.
'So what are you up to, Bill?
Tom Burnett. – No, I kissed it good-bye
When my liver went up the creek:
Had to settle for this instead;
You still have the company, like.
– Harry Clough? Nice fellow. He's dead.'

It went on for an hour, about,
To the point where a half-known face
Shoved itself forward to shout,
'This beer's a bloody disgrace,
And you can't even get bloody served!'
Jim coped. The chap who had been
Young Taylor was quite well preserved,
Though his jowls were a little wan.

That was sort of the signal for scoff;
'It shows you how things have changed:
Back then, he'd have had to fuck off
Or get handled,' – Perkins had ranged
His cardboard plate next to mine –
'But you can't really do that now,
And it isn't just auld lang syne;
As if we've grown up, somehow.'

Clifford Perkins (Slosher as was)
Said society's values were more
And more unencumbered, because
No bugger could save the entire
Class structure from final decay.
I waited for Jim to respond
In the old familiar way,
But he nodded and smiled and yawned.

With the coffee and cake and cakes
Came the speeches, which finally squashed
A discussion of heart-attacks;
The first on his feet was sloshed,
And Jim had him off them again,
Quite politely, in five seconds flat.
This would all have been funny then,
I said to myself, or it might.

The second and third and the rest
Stood sober enough and to spare
On things like the lately deceased
And how lucky we were to be there;
I was turning my thoughts to booze
When that side of it came to an end:
Ex-major MacClure – 'Cheers, boys!' –
Had realised his hope to attend.

He had changed very little: he wore
Bifocals now, but his face
Was as sharply defined as before,
His hair still abundant; his voice
Was the same semi-muted shout
When he talked, as he did for a while,
Of blokes I knew nothing about;
And, by God, he had kept up his style.

I finally got a word through:
Had he run into Nicholls at all?
(A privilege granted to few
Is meeting a pratt on the scale
Of Nicholls: by common consent
A nitwit not fit to shift shit;
Whether more of a bastard or cunt,
Views varied, one has to admit.)

None who saw it could ever forget
MacClure as he took Nicholls off:
Him bumming your last cigarette,
His frown, then his clangorous laugh,
But now, as I mentioned the name
And a bunch of us stood at the bar,
Sandy announced with aplomb
That they met now and then for a jar.

Disbelief, rather broadly expressed,
Was called for, but not even Jim
Seemed shocked or surprised in the least,
So I said, 'A jar with *him*?
You must be out of your – hey!
I remember you swearing, back then,
They could come and take you away
If you ever drank with him for fun.'

'Oh yes?' said MacClure. 'Well, you know
How it is – you exaggerate. And
It was all a long time ago;
Now we're older, we understand
Other blokes, or some of us do.
One thing about Nicholls, Bill,
He always stuck up for you,
And you needed a spot of goodwill.'

He spoke at his customary pitch,
And with his customary grin.
Not much later, Jim looked at his watch
And mentioned packing it in.
No one suggested a song –
Well, no one still there was tight,
And the lads started getting along
(Bar those booked in for the night).

III
What had brought us together before
Was over, no doubt about that;
What had held us together was more
Than, whether you liked it or not,
Going after a single aim,
One procedure laid down from above;
In their dozens, no two the same,
Small kinds and degrees of love.

And that was quite natural then,
When to do what we had to do
Showed us off perfectly, when
We were not so much young as new,
With some shine still on us, unmarked
(At least only mildly frayed),
When everything in us worked,
And no allowances made.

So, when one of us had his leave stopped,
Was awarded a dose of the clap
Or an extra guard, or was dropped
Up to his ears in the crap,
Or felt plain bloody browned off,
He never got left on his own:
The others had muscle enough
To see that he soldiered on.

Disbandment has come to us
As it comes to all who grow old;
Demobilised now, we face
What we faced when we first enrolled.
Stand still in the middle rank!
See you show them a touch of pride –
Left-right, left-right, bags of swank –
On the one-man pass-out parade.

John Ash

TRISTAN: AUTUMN 1938

Tristan! Tristan!
Where is he? Damn him!
The woman lies back on the bed.
Leaves blotch the lawn
like discolorations on old skin.
The garden furniture looks uneasy
like night-beasts caught out in daylight;
it rusts and splinters . . .
                                        The house
an unconvincing backdrop, grandiose and damp –
its face-pack peeling; her apartment,
an island among desolated salons
cluttered with screens and mirrors,
cosmetics, kimonos and globe lamps:
a gramophone spills out vapid, masochistic vocals
and mooning saxophones
tinged with the needle's acid hiss.

She lies half-naked on the bed,
calls for her chauffeur, lover and dealer
who brings her morphine. Tristan!
Tristan, who observes with distaste her slack flesh.

It is today she visits the asylum. The wind is high, –
leaves lash the car, –
it has inspired her husband to rhetorical verse
invoking destiny and freedom, abusing the State.
(He has behaved well –
he does not need restraints today: his doctors admire
the curative properties of Art.) Their son,
she informs him, is marrying
a perfectly brainless daughter of the petit bourgeoisie,
and, despite that story involving her uncle,
a perfectly conventional one. It is an act of revolt!
Her husband still gabbles his Aeolian declamation
making wide gestures towards an audience
of winding sheets suspended in an amphitheatre of ice.

Driving home, she feels preoccupied, depressed –
her husband, her faltering heart (once
she almost died) her intractable son
who insults her, who hates poor Tristan, O, Tristan
the marvellous strong column of his neck,
his hard thighs, – exquisite brute! Arriving home,
– forlorn! The porch roof is leaking;
windowframes bulge and sag;
roots are prizing the steps apart
and the finial Sphinx lost its nose years ago,
why, even before her sister Giulietta's death.

It must end; she can bear it no longer.
The place stinks. Stinks!
She will sell the house, sell everything!
She must pack. Tristan is a born adventurer.
How they will travel, –
beyond the clichés of casinos, hotels and esplanades, –
beyond civilisation! She imagines
the Nile, the pyramids at Meroe, the Amazon,
the Opera House at Manaus . . .

In these places she will be appreciated:
she will appear an aristocrat, dazzling the outposts
with the dying light of her once famous beauty,
her unflagging sophistication, –
ambassadress for no country,
but of the highest Culture and couture!
And Tristan will protect her
(in those places men will find her irresistible). She must
    pack –

This place stinks! Leaves cling. Curtains catch.
Windows stick, stick . . . Tristan!
The car is ready, the trunks packed; the phone rings.
She reaches for the receiver: a sudden pain
blinds her and she falls.
The receiver hangs, whispers and goes dead.
Tristan, Tristan . . .
                        Tristan
waits by the car in his beautiful white uniform.
She does not come down.
Evening falls. He waits, –
a neglected statue; she does not come down:
the car horn answers itself from the boarded windows.

George Barker

THE WATERFALL OF VYRNWY

What, my dear Hedley, are we doing here at
this source of water falling from so high that
it might have found its fount among clouds in which no
artisan had a hand? And why with two
small children who do not so much ride on the shoulders
of rocks as flitter round about the fallen boulders
not seeking, as we do, some sense of origins hidden here
but having found it? What is this sense of origins they have found
here among the murmurations and soliliquies of that sound
you and I know the poem takes its fountaining inception
from? I think it possible that this perception
consists of the logos at the heart of all natural facts
as forgiveness finally presides over all human acts
and as the pathway through the Commission-conifered forest
began among beds in which the newborn child first
saw the Gardens of Babylon hanging in the air. How
can I ask why you, Hedley, and I are here now
when all that I know is simply that we are
here seeking among the fallen gardens and water falling for
the knowledge of why we are here? We search among
the stones and elisons of water and reflections what long
we shall seek and not find, the impulse of
that recurring and continual suicide of love
like this small cataract that rides to the crest of the mountain
and casts itself over to create the poem and the fountain.

W. E. A. COURSE

This evening we are doing Pasternak.
Last week we did Alexander Solzhenitsyn.
Outside this room which has wall to wall carpets
And stands illuminated in its own grounds,
The English autumn dies, modest and well-mannered,
The leaves swept away from the drive, the sun still warm
During the daylight hours, warmth reflected upon the face
Of our tutor, who could be my son, and looks like
D. H. Lawrence.
They should have warned me of Simochka
Who sits on my right in fashionable clothes,
And long blond hair, or Nerzhin,
Who was transferred at the end of Chapter nine.
We sit in a circle, but Dante would not have recognised us
As persons with grave and tranquil eyes and great
Authority in our carriage and attitude.
This proves we have actually read The First Circle,
But this week I am glad to have travelled
The long train journey without Omar Sharif,
And seen the candles burn, and the iced rowanberries.
Across the room sits Lara, rather silent and also
A librarian, and next to her the Public Prosecutor.
Outside the wind is blowing, and the snow blocks out
This commuter town, silting against the door.
We are trapped, we cannot escape, we grovel
For a few potatoes, a few logs of wood.
Red specks and threads of blood gleam on the snow,
And the sound of gun-fire ends the class as we flee
In cars and on bicycles with our books under our arms.
Next week to Sicily with Lampedusa,
Nunc et in hora mortis nostrae. Amen,
And I shall be cast for the Leopard's wife,
Gesummaria, how far away the snow will seem.

It will be hot wherever we are, and Bendico
Will follow me home through the neon-lighted streets,
His dust will crumble and his smell pursue me,
As Komarovsky pursues me now, in his green car,
Dark as the forests at Varykino, cold as a Russian
Winter, in this Michaelmas weather, cruel and ruthless
As the unseasonable revolution we are all waiting for,
With only a grammar of feeling to defend us.
Ah, Yury, the snow is falling, the stars have gone,
And I am alone; we are lost to each other forever.

Patricia Beer

THE BLACK HALO

The halo of Judas is black, blacker than nightfall,
The disciple has started to teach
Leading the way
Pointing out his master to the keen killers
Their helmets sweating in the dark air
Their pikes sticking into the sky like fireworks.

The soldiers are preceded
By gentlemen from the city,
Dignitaries in velvet, a torch guiding them,
Charmed to capture the rebel and restore order,
Charmed to have found a traitor to do the kissing.

Eleven gold haloes circling eleven good faces
Jut into the crowd unsympathetically
Wearing a look-at-me nursery expression.

How shocking is the black halo of the traitor
Which blinked out at the touch of skin,
Brilliant as any till the deadly greeting.
It could not disappear, be the plain air
Round the head of an unimportant man.

Jesus looks as red and smug as an apple
Judas is a fox but would eat anything
They cling to each other
They depend on each other.

All this the bystander can see for himself.
The book has told us the sequel:
His goodness charred, he took leave
And hanged himself from a tree.
See his black halo crouching
Up in the leaves like a black cat.

Connie Bensley

FEBRUARY

February – a poor month for the foot fetishist:
Wellingtons, old clodhoppers,
Socks that have almost breathed their last.
And when the occasional foot is glimpsed, naked,
By the determined voyeur,
It is deathly pale and flabby,
Contoured and moulded by the winter boot,
And, though fascinating,
Hardly contemporary –
More like something unearthed from a previous season.

But dream hotly, you fellow fetishists,
Of a spell in March,
When the weather may break, and evoke
The first disturbing sandals of the year.

James Berry

MOMENT OF LOVE

Sweetrose Sweetrose you pretty
Lawd Lawd hol' this time
hol' it like Joshua still the sun
She lyin' here I full
I brimful with joy
   brimful with joy
no empty pocket on me to drag me
no lockedhead of mine to fail me
no government debate to bug me
Only she lyin' here needin' not a word
An' I sing sweeter than any black bird
Sweetrose Sweetrose you pretty
Stay good an' don't get baby
   Stay good an' don't get baby

Thomas Blackburn

DOLOMITE

Some five steep miles from the old town of Belluno,
At the Casa Bortot we drank wine and looked at the river, Piave,
Humming in silence on the afternoon of Italian summer,
Then heaved on our packs and started for the rifugio.
The climbers' track ran high over a stream from the mountain,
Its stones polished by winter's great water
Fuming down from the glacier of the Schiara,
As we sweated in the scent of pines and the gentian.

Then, after two hours, the track ran down to
A flatness of the stream-bed where we drank and rested
And I smeared our feet with soap as you said they ached,
Then the last precipitous, grinding hour to the rifugio.
It was dusk when we reached it and heard the sound of voices
Of three or four Austrians smoking on the balcony –
'*Grüss Gott*' – then we met the custodian and his wife and their
    baby,
At seeing old friends one rejoices.

That night we were woken up by the glare of lightning
And got out of our bunks to watch it illuminate
Each detail of the orange, enormous Dolomite
But there was no thunder to suggest storm and giants fighting
And at five o'clock we ate bread and drank black coffee.
It must be twenty years now but the details are insoluble,
And death will not blur the customary that is memorable,
And you were then, as this night, most beautiful to me.

On the way to the climb and its start by the Portala,
Black lizards crawled too repulsive to be eaten by living creature
And I recall picking out the particular feature
For which we were using the Via Ferrata, Il Gusella della Schiara,
The meaning of being then and our destiny
The 'crux' of the mountain and some two hundred feet high.
Far below we heard the bells of grazing sheep.

On the top of the needle that was by no means easy,
Guides had riveted a cross of iron,
Memento of our situation and destination.
We reached the slabs again by a third abseil,
And walked down to the hut after reclimbing the Via Ferrata,
In the high, solar glare of the later noon.
Never again will I step so lightly under this sun;
Before we ate and drank wine we took stinging grappa.

Strange how some moments that were 'now' can never finish.
Here I blend a climb out of many climbs that illuminated
The monotony of events long gone and quite faded,
But these like love, communion, art, do not perish.
And so on my sixtieth birthday I celebrate the instant,
That has no end to its ceremony of delight –
We mean we are nearer the dawn when we say 'It's late';
Where is there an end to it, the imperdurable moment?

Peter Bland

LAMENT FOR A LOST GENERATION

Between V-J Day and 1951
we wore our first grey longs.
Drab, insular, short of vitamin C,
much given to fags and the fumbled grope

we became – like prefabs
or the last steam train –
something slightly embarrassing
that goes on and on: fodder for talks like

The Ration-Book Age or
The Wartime Growth of the Working Mum.
We were few; conceived in the slump;
brought up in shelters and under the stairs;

eleven-plus boys; post-war conscripts
who lowered the flag on better days.
What we lacked was a style!
We were make-do-and-menders,

utility-grey men, the last of a line.
You can tell us a mile off, even now;
there's a touch of austerity
under the eyes; a hint of carbolic

in our after-shave; a lasting doubt
about the next good time.

Ian Bowman

LAST LINES

An eldrich skreich,
aich o' the past;
the pantin' sough
o' a simmerin' boiler;
a smoor o' steam
abin the auld brig –
ghaist in the sunshine.
Whitna ferlie's this?
There's nae train rin
ablow the auld brig
this ten year syne.
But yin's there noo:
no much o' a train –
a muckle black engine
snorin' like a whale;
a wheen flat trucks
clinkin' at the couplin's.
Nae like the wee smart tanks
licht broon an' polished brass
wi' sax coaches ahint,
skelpin' doon through the cuttin'
past the bricht banks o' floo'rs
an' trim palings, tae the bield
o' the station's canopy.
A' the village on the platform –
cantie auld folk, callants an' hizzies,
weans an' dugs – even the minister
(wi'oot his dog-collar) –
a richt horoyallie,
awa' tae Craigendoran
fur a sail doon the Clyde
on the Jeanie Deans.

They're singin' already
tae Wull's accordion,
an twa-three rinnin'
frae the Craigen Glen
wi' last-minute bottles.
That's a' deid noo.
Aye, deid – but no' buriet
yet.

Thon muckle black engine,
it's the undertaker.
The wheen o' flat trucks,
it's the dolefu' hearse.
They're howkin' up the line,
cawin' at the deid rails,
coupin' them intil the trucks.
Nae laggin', jist a steady
slow gait doon the cuttin',
whaur nae train will ever
come skelpin' again.
It's the funeral jaunt,
dreich, wi'oot floo'rs;
nae mourners, nae minister
tae say the last words:
only the sterk skreich
o' the engine's whistle.

Edwin Brock

THE DEATH OF MICE AND
THE PAIN OF MEN

I liked her to speak in George's voice.
'Tell me again' I'd say to her
feeling the still-warm mouse
in my jacket pocket. And as she spoke
the heavy tires on the steel roads
grew louder; there were voices
among the trees and at times
the dry barking of pulling dogs.

'Tell me about the alfalfa for
the rabbits' I said. 'And who
will collect the brown and speckled eggs.'
The mouse in my pocket was shedding
fleas: soon it would be hard
and old and cold. 'Tell me
about the thunderstorm' I said.

George, I am not proud of this: I have
to dig for details, even guess. I want
to hear how long it took to show him
any word would be enough. I want to know
when he began to grow with the luck
that had caught him up.

'You'd love Switzerland' you said.
'Below the snowline there's alfalfa
grass for rabbits, and hens hide
the brown and speckled eggs we'd find
for breakfast. Always a storm is
brewing and the party is trapped in
sleeping bags in some Swiss chalet.
And there are voices in the night
joining mouths and skin to one idea
which rushes to a pre-determined end.'

Now the mouse in my pocket is as squashed
and red as you were George. And my jacket
is as tell-tale as the sheets that you both
smuggled from your bed into another room.
George, does your joy hurt me, or do I enjoy
the pain that he knew only as joy? Which
of these goes deeper?

God, my head is hurting again, and there
are people in the woods. Why does everybody
in all the stories always escape to Switzerland?
Is that where we are going George? Is there
a storm brewing for us? Are we now trapped
in some Swiss chalet? And will we
wave our warm red sheets
from out of an upstairs window?

Balfour Brown

WINGMAN

We have quite a stack of pictures here, gentlemen –
would it be right you wouldn't want to see them all?

Well, here we see initial conversion
with breastbone sawn out and ribs
opened up barn-door fashion but heart
lungs etcetera in normal position.

Yes, General, I have been in a barn.

Now this shot looks kind of similar
but the blood vessels have been rerouted
and you'll notice the lungs have been swung
upward parallel with the shoulder line.
Please observe the cavities thus obtained.

Here's the same subject after death
with chest replacement wall in position –
the wall you're looking at is a prototype
without bomb cavities or engine mounts.

Should we skip some shots, gentlemen?

Now here we have
number one successful conversion.
As you can see, the integral wing
looks wide as a church door. Yet,
with micro heart, chest depth
averages one-point-three inches.

And, hullo! he could still feel
like horsing around.

We have full assembly. We have full assembly.
The leg coffining is the same
ceramic material as the chest wall.

Should we kind of flick through these
close shots? The stanchions from engines
to chest mounts. Left or right lungspace
with war pack. Decal. Which does not
read LOM. Which reads el theta em
named for elasmothorax missile.

No, General, he flies feet first.

There is no landing gear, General.

Alan Brownjohn

A NIGHT IN THE GAZEBO

I
Look down into hotels where girls work
   In their vacations,
And in the early evening, managers, averaging
Forty-six years old, induce them to upper bedrooms,
Empty because business is dropping off:
Think of the protestations round the coasts of England,
The moaning on the candlewick coverlets,
And the girls so young, this the first time for most of them,
And the managers cautious and honourable,
Saying they won't go too far, and going
Too far, the girls done with A Levels,
And the managers pressing and leering and the minds blown for
                                    days.

II
Look down at one manager at seven-thirty, all his girls
   Heltering through his mind,
And fewer girls each year in the last three years,
But this year more girls than for three years past,
Five girls to be exact, so it is spring once more
And the blood sparkles, at an average age
Of forty-six. There he is now, leering in the glass
Behind the lounge bar, tilting, adroitly, Chartreuse,
Thinking of his five girls this season: Tina, Prue,
And Elaine, and Kirsten, who pulled the scarlet
Curtains herself, and Rosemary, queen of impermeable
Silence, who will come back of her own accord.

III
Look down there at the window of a room at dusk
   Where a pensive manager,
Letting the twilight change to dark, sits alone
Without a light at nine-thirty, run out of cigarettes,
Sits alone, eyes open, in a crumbling swivel chair.

Now he hears the feeble whine of a slow lift,
And a girl comes in who understands his sadness,
Business declining and years declining
– And a good love quickens in this very young girl,
Or a love upgraded from pity (she has brought some cigarettes)
For a manager pining heavily in a hotel
Not doing particularly well . . .

IV
Look down at a boy friend emptying fruit machines
    On the pier at ten-fifteen,
After a fair day's business. The ogling machines
Are adjusted finely to concede just a little
And grasp the rest to themselves,
And his girl is adjusted finely in the same way
– Because of a manager of a hotel (where they
Spend the early evenings in an upper bedroom.)
She is meeting the boy in the Bull, and
For him life feels like a nasty row
Of mocking variables, apples, plums and flags,
As he filches the coins with which he will buy the drinks.

V
And look at this boy friend at midnight
    At the girl's gate:
Now cradling the sobbing girl, who has told him
Everything all at once in a sudden gush.
She says she could be sick, which she could not,
And the boy is sick instead because it has taken
Eleven pale ales to her four bacardis-and-coke
To bring her to this point of revelation.
Thus: the manager, his girl friend, and her boy friend –
It's a bad time for all of them (though at this moment a letter
Is on its way to the girl to say she has
Two D's and an E and a place at the North-East Polytechnic.)

VI

But look again at this boy friend, who is feeling better
    Up the hill past the Cats' Home
On his long walk back about an hour later.
He is compassionating the manager in question,
Whose letters he has been shown: 'Dear Tina,
I long for you all the time . . .' and similar things.
He can guess the timeless agony of the man,
Longing so much for the girl he more or less
Longs for himself, and he is not so jealous.
He could be in the same position one day.
He could be in the same . . . He is overcome
With a selfless presagement of the nastiness of time.

VII

Look between the chink in the curtains
    In one hotel window,
Where a manager, at one-thirty, is turning a coverlet
Down, the only coverlet he ever turns
Down, to slink into bed beside his wife.
Groping the pillow in the darkness, this manager
Thinks of that day's baffling girl: 'You've never
Read any Gary Snyder or Frantz Fanon, you've hardly
Heard of Claes Oldenburg or Roland Barthes,
Or of Simon or Garfunkel,' she had said in reproach,
'Do you call that living? – 'Yes,' he thinks,
As he thinks of her left breast flipping the back of his knee.

VIII

In the terrible small hours look over
    Everyone fitfully asleep,
And do not imagine they do not have complex dreams.
E.g., a girl is at the bottom of a slimy pit
With smooth sides, and hairy managers are toppling
Hairy managers in rockers' goggles down on her,

So that she screams; only the scream
Comes out a bit ecstatically and she can't
Explain to herself why this should be really so,
Or how she should have come to be here at all.
It stays with her while she dresses for another
Long day at the hotel. She can't wait for the early evening to
come round.

IX

Look into a corridor where a girl at nine-twenty a.m.
Walks carrying sheets,
And a second follows, to shake them out with her,
One girl moderately appealing and the other
Less appealing than her, not least in her perceptions
(Which she keeps to herself.) The conversation
Is equivocal, since they are discussing the manager
And the first girl has more to disclose than she says,
Though she is hinting, continually hinting,
In the faint breeze from the sheets. Small tabs with
Laundry numbers fall off the outflung linen,
And the bedroom radio sings of *leurs déguisements fantasques*.

X

Lastly, gaze out there at the crematorium.
Having consumed fourteen
Tequilas in half-an-hour, a manager
Is being consumed to rest. His wife comes first,
And behind her follow forty-six girls in all,
The youngest sixteen, the oldest thirty-four,
And all in states of nostalgia or raw distress
According to how lately they knew the man.
So wife and girls compassionate each other
As the clergyman, noting an ancient English
Ritual of mourning, shakes each girl by the hand.
If this can happen, the world must be good. It is ten forty-five.

46

Carol Bruggen

GOOD-BYE TO ALAN

The coroner's officer, calm, matter-of-fact,
writes with a beautiful hand. The widow sits.
Coldly with clarity he writes and asks
Rita the questions now not relevant.
Upright and white she gives the detailed facts
as though reciting last week's laundry list.

Square and unmoved sunlight cools the desk,
coroner's officer filling endless forms
writing about the deceased in stilted terms
which would have stirred the sly and sideways smile,
crinkled the shrewd, long look and lit the light
in the deceased's blue penetrating eyes.

A mortuary attendant falters in
wearing a dark, neat overall. He lays
objects from Alan's pockets on the desk.
Next to the tattered wallet, cheque-book stub,
newspage cuttings, letters, pile of coins
desolate spread two unofficial tears.

Rita picks the used possessions up
and puts them in her handbag one by one.
Upright and white she sits and the officer,
labouring, puts on record her dry, bleached grief.
Raising his head he smiles a sad, small smile,
speaks to her quietly, opens a door,

leads her into a chapel, dusky, filled
with a high bier. Alan, moulded, lies
under a velvet cloth of faded blue.
Sun from the tiny window panes drifts in,
slants on his turned face, still mobility.
He doesn't seem asleep: he's active nerve.

Gone from the sunlight his untidiness,
uncontrollable shirts he always wore,
trousers with splits and shoes with gaping holes,
hair blown wild around his quizzical face.
He's like a man who went about disguised,
nothing is left but the order from beneath.

Nothing is left but his motive, strong, direct,
nothing is left but his white-hot, vivid course.
Nothing is left of Alan but intense,
vigorous creativity; alive
buried below his action, now in death
shown transparent on his questing face.

Stumbling and speechless Rita leaves the morgue,
walks past the hospital, upright and white,
walks past the red brick walls, the new-leaf trees,
faint in the warm air, sits in his shambling car,
turns with a moan remembering she didn't say
good-bye to Alan, his gleaming, distant corpse.

Jim Burns

BONAPARTE'S RETREAT

Christ, all that snow!
Miles and miles of it
everywhere you looked,
and the silly bitch
I had with me said she
liked it, everything
seemed so pure and clean.
She was only facing
her front, of course,
and the fur hood stopped
her seeing the strangers
menacing our flanks.
And she thought that
glancing back would bring
bad luck, and that's
why she never saw the
trail of blood marking
the route we'd taken.
She said she loved snow,
it levelled everything,
made it neat and tidy,
but I knew it would be
the death of us, it was
so damned hard to push
our feet through,
and if you went down
it covered you at once.
So, there we were, lost,
things coming apart,
and she chattered about
how nice it all was,
and the snow just kept on
falling and falling.

Jim Burns

SETTLING A DEBT

She stopped me in the street,
and said I owed her something.
There's a wise woman for you,
one who knows that a whore
deserves her just dues.

Jack Carey

From THE BLACK RABBIT AND
THE MANTRA

7

Laconic rabbit, aerial ears early
warners, your nose judges – you sniff the world
and smell that it is good.
                              I love your listener's
silence tuned to pure earth vibrations.
Nobody should make you clumsy with words.
Your running is a down-to-earth flying.

Only extremes tear a voice out of you,
and I have heard you hiss softly inside yourself
as if the silence had its own menacing sound.

You line your burrow with blue fur, you make
the whole earth a drum warning against the sky
death angel, like the dumb girl in *Mother Courage*.

8

The onion heat is all in the stalk.

Once I bent to look at the purple blur
of a chopped chive head. I saw
massed crystal petals with sharp points
clustered in numbers of six, each one
with a thin dark spine down the middle.
At the bottom of each cup depths of whiteness blurred.

Also, I have awakened in the morning to new-born
clouds of stars drifting in and out of light by violet
flowered curtains, which my coping day-spectacles
focused to dust hairs thickening near my head.

9

The thick muscle of a heart still beating
when there is no heart . . .

The head asking, What is the point, what is the point?

The heart booms, blood swooshes through pipes;
magnified, pores are wonderland peepshow caves,
the oesophagus tunnelling deep down.

We don't look at each other's middle-aged
nakedness, preferring to touch in the dark.
The impulse flickers, and all those kite-tailed sperm
are dying for a lost cause in a foreign tunnel.

Seeing how the arrivers ram the eggshell fortress,
I think, 'The sperm is a born kamikaze rapist,'
but you say, 'It is the Sleeping Beauty myth.'

Charles Causley

SINGING GAME

The Round House, c. 1830, is built over a broken
market cross at Newport, Launceston, in Cornwall.

Here we go round the Round House
In the month of one,
Looking to the eastward
For the springing sun.
The sky is made of ashes,
The trees are made of bone,
And all the water in the well
Is stubborn as a stone.

Here we go round the Round House
In the month of two
Waiting for the weather
To thaw my dancing shoe.
In St Thomas River
Hide the freckled trout,
But for dinner on Friday
I shall pull one out.

Here we go round the Round House
In the month of three,
Listening for the bumble
Of the humble-bee.
The light is growing longer,
The geese begin to lay,
The song-thrush in the church-yard
Charms the cold away.

Here we go round the Round House
In the month of four,
Watching a couple dressed in green
Dancing through the door.

One wears a wreath of myrtle,
Another, buds of thorn:
God grant that all men's children
Be as sweetly born.

Here we go round the Round House
In the month of five,
Waiting for the summer
To tell us we're alive.
All round the country
The warm seas flow,
The devil's on an ice-cap
Melting with the snow.

Here we go round the Round House
In the month of six;
High in the tower
The town clock ticks.
Hear the black quarter-jacks
Beat the noon bell;
They say the day is half away
And the year as well.

Here we go round the Round House
In the month of seven,
The river running thirsty
From Cornwall to Devon.
The sun is on the hedgerow
The cattle in the stream,
And one will give us strawberries
And one will give us cream.

Here we go round the Round House
In the month of eight
Hoping that for harvest
We shall never wait.
Slyly the sunshine
Butters up the bread
To bear us through the winter
When the light is dead.

Here we go round the Round House
In the month of nine,
Watching the orchard apple
Turning into wine.
The day after tomorrow
I'll take one from the tree
And pray the worm will do no harm
If it comes close to me.

Here we go round the Round House
In the month of ten
While the cattle winter
In the farmer's pen.
Thick the leaves are lying
On the coppice floor;
Such a coat against the cold
Never a body wore.

Here we go round the Round House
In the month of eleven,
The sea-birds swiftly flying
To the coast of heaven.
The plough is in the furrow,
The boat is on the strand;
May I be fed on fish and bread
While water lies on land.

Here we go round the Round House
In the month of twelve,
The hedgers break the brier
And the ditchers delve.
As we go round the Round House
May the moon and sun
Guide us to tomorrow
And the month of one:
And life be never done.

Cal Clothier

JUST SO STORY

Oh, Best Beloved, I'm sorry to say
The last elephant died today –
After forty years on public view,
Dear old Nelly, the pride of the zoo,
Finally snuffed it, and no amount
Of antibiotics could beat the count.

The Last Elephant – what an honour! –
And think of the care we've lavished on her:
A million hours of audio-tape
(Which is more than we gave the last ape),
So every rumble and every fart,
Every beat of her dear old heart,
Is in the can, with a year or two
Of continuous film, so that we can view
Every hour of her life long after she
Has made her peace with Eternity.

Creatively stuffed and coated in plastic
To keep her old skin as taut as elastic
(Towards the end she was looking baggy,
Her trunk like putty, her cheeks all saggy),
Nelly will stand to the end of time
In our Wild Museum, for ever prime,
Rescued at last from the wear and tear
Of evolution, by sterile air –
Immortal and visible ever more,
Nelly will rank with the Dinosaur.
And this, oh, Best Beloved, just shows
That Man *can* cherish what Nature bestows.

Stewart Conn

WITNESSES

Jehovah's Witnesses have been, and gone;
Their steel rims flashing in the sun.

Some sixth sense warned me to remain
Under cover, till I had seen

Who was at the door. They were
Persuasive as ever: 'Prepare

To act on the good news.' 'Can you envisage
A future without God?' 'It is our privilege

To invite you to partake of His banquet. . . .'
Our upstairs neighbour, firm but discreet,

Closes the door. Father of two young children,
Mine is a different desperation.

I sit tight in my sense of sin.
Their dark figures diminish, in the sun.

Rosalind Conway

MY FATHER

Where his cats
boltinstraightforthekitchen
love pours pungently
from little 'gourmet' tins
and large 'serve with love' boxes.

'All you can eat!'
the plump house boasts.

Coming home
I'm overwhelmed
by frozen legs of lamb,
pecan pies, steaks,
the fridge, the freezer
jammed full:
a turkey has given its life
for me, and lies
upside-down
but poised and swell-chested.

I love you – I know you
are telling me this
in your way,
but I can't become
your fat cat
living from lap to kitchen.

Elsie Cranmer

POPULARITY

He was a man shunned by most,
Not very lovable, perhaps,
Because of a certain taciturnity
And a certain cleverness
Which barred him from the company of fools.
'He is a snob,' they said,
'Always alone, so strange,' they said.

One night he died, so suddenly
They were quite proud,
'We knew him very well,' they said,
'He was a friend to all,' they said.

He could not contradict them, being dead.

Adele David

TRIPTYCH

I am the one in the middle
without room for expansion.
It is the station
of the wild honey life,
of the scent of white lilac,
of time compressed
into standstill.
I am learning my parents.
Am one with the present pale colours:
even the apples this year come in yellows.

I am her mother in the right.
She is still the one in the middle.
She says, 'She is the station
of the piled money life,
of the Lent of 'white lilac'.
I say she is mad.

I am her father. I am left.
You were once my little daughter sitting on my knee.
You were pretty then and happy.
'My Doll,' I called you, 'Doll.'
Now you are far too big and distant:
I am growing old away from the taste of apples.

Douglas Dunn

ON HER PICTURE LEFT WITH HIM

On trains to London and the south
   And thus away from me
These words in my enamoured mouth
   Summon the flattery
Of who it is and what I love,
   Distracting me.

Lady, so far outside, and gone,
   Your picture left with me
Is like the world I look upon
   And shows reality
As who it is and why I love,
   Distracting me.

Thus do I gaze on you, and drink
   Your face you left with me,
And speak to you in whispered ink
   With that humility
Which is a lesser spoil of love,
   Distracting me.

Now is the afternoon turned round
   To dusk that darkens me,
And walking on nocturnal ground
   Offers no liberty
From who I am and who I love,
   Distracting me.

D. J. Enright

ANTHROPOS FEELS HIS AGE

Anthropos has lived a long time
And many lives. Chieftain and pedant,
Merchant and peasant. Has borne children,
And arms, and filled long cemeteries.

Anthropos feels weary, though he can ride
In a car, a tractor will pull his plough,
And machines add up and take away.
They also multiply.

He has fewer things to hide from.
(The sabre-toothed tiger has left,
There are laws against drunken driving,
The Black Death has been abolished,
Religions are not supposed to burn him.)

But there are fewer places to hide.
Once there were torrents to cross,
Forests to explore, and the nature of God.
The objects that squat on his desk
Afford him no refuge.

Television shows him places to hide,
Where he cannot lose himself.
He is versed in the anatomy of man
And the biology of woman. The world
Is full of good intentions and dislike.

Anthropos looks at the moon:
It is pretty from a distance.
The sabre-toothed tiger is not found there.
Nor thrilling and dreadful women. Nor gods.
Machines love it.

Anthropos feels he has lived too long,
Or else not long enough.
He can turn petulant at any moment
And throw things about.
Then he will have to put them back.

U. A. Fanthorpe

POEM FOR OSCAR WILDE

Lane is cutting cucumber
Sandwiches, and the dogcart
Is coming round at the same
Time next week. The weather
Continues charming.

Reading Gaol and seedy France
Lurk in Cecily's garden
Under the pink roses. As
A man sows, so let him reap.
This truth is rarely pure,
And never simple.

Babies, handbags and lives are
Abandoned (I use the word
In the sense of *lost* or *mislaid*).
Sin, a temperance beverage,
Has stained somebody's lining.

This exquisite egg, which hatched
Ruin for you, who made it,
Retains its delicate poise.
Grief turns hair gold, and teacake
Becomes tragic. The weather
Continues charming.

Elaine Feinstein

DAD

Your old hat hurts me, and those black
   fat raisins you liked to press into
my palm from your soft heavy hand:
   I see you staggering back up the path
with sacks of potatoes from some local farm,
   fresh eggs, flowers. Every day I grieve

for your great heart broken and you gone.
   You loved to watch the trees. This year
you did not see their Spring.
   The sky was freezing over the fen
as on that somewhere secretly appointed day
   you beached: cold, white-faced, shivering.

What happened, old bull, my loyal
   hoarse-voiced warrior? The hammer
blow that stopped you in your track
   and brought you to a hospital monitor
could not destroy your courage
   to the end you were
uncowed and unconcerned with pleasing anyone.

I think of you now as once again safely
   at my mother's side, the earth as
chosen as a bed, and feel most sorrow for
   all that was gentle in
my childhood buried there
   already forfeit, now forever lost.

James Fenton and John Fuller

POEM AGAINST CATHOLICS

The boring executors approach their locks,
Fumbling with keys and more than half-way dense:
Sylvia Plath is given to C. B. Cox,
Lawrence to Leavis, Pope to Joseph Spence,
Pound to *Agenda*, Eliot to his wife,
Hopkins to Bridges and Kafka to Max Brod –
But Jesus gave the *Church* eternal life!
God we hate Catholics and their Catholic God.

It isn't that we'd rather someone who
Instead of singing simply *says* you it.
The whole palaver simply isn't *true*.
We'd not *prefer* a Quaker to a Jesuit.
But in the Proselytising Handicap
The odds are even where they ride roughshod
And drive their spurs into the suffering map.
God we hate Catholics and their Catholic God.

Graham Greene finds them everywhere he travels
With submachineguns underneath their cassocks.
You can be certain, as the plot unravels,
They're smuggling opium in knee-worn hassocks.
Police-chiefs quote Pascal. Priests hit the bottle.
Strong men repent in Nishni-Novgorod.
The whole *galère* one could with pleasure throttle.
God we hate Catholics and their Catholic God.

The object of their worship makes us *cross*,
Since their employment of it is so gainful.
They sold it off like bits of candy-floss.
(Surely the Romans meant it to be painful?)
Their tortured idols are so psychedelic
With gold and lapis artwork *à la mode*,
And nearly every thumbscrew is a relic.
God we hate Catholics and their Catholic goad.

They call their horrid children after saints
And educate them by such dubious means
They eagerly succumb to strange complaints
Or turn psychotic in their early teens.
'Ursula worries me,' exclaims her mother.
'Her manner recently has been so odd.
I've *told* her she must *not* cremate her brother.'
God we hate Catholics and their Catholic God.

See in the summerhouse where Father Flynn
Fingers his rosary and sets to work
Explaining why the church holds it a sin:
'You mustn't ever hold it. That's called jerk-
ing off. Six *mea culpas*, Benedict.'
He's coaching him for Ampleforth, poor sod.
He'll get some education, we predict.
God we hate Catholics and their Catholic God.

'Not now,' cries Mrs Macnamara, '*later*!'
When leapt on by her husband (what a beast).
'It says so on my Catholic calculator.
It also says so on my Catholic priest.'
She'd do much better with a mortal coil
To spoil the child and spare the husband's rod.
Why don't they put a bill through in the Dáil?
God we hate Catholics and their Catholic God.

Their sheer resourcefulness one can't disparage.
External Combustion was their own invention,
So (indisputably) divorceless marriage
Which like a sardine key creates some tension.
But *only once*. What moral supermen!
Or else what Paul said must have been a cod
Since those who marry twice must burn again.
God we hate Catholics and their Catholic God.

Rich English Catholics, busy doing good work
For filthy mission schools in fascist states.
Oily confessors crawling from the woodwork
With first-class tickets to the pearly gates.
How nice that Lady Priesthole looks so well.
She's left her housemaid's knee behind in Lourdes.
But where's the housemaid? God alone can tell.
God we hate Catholics and their Catholic Gourdes.

High Anglo-Catholics are beneath contempt –
All intellectual and moral wrecks.
They love the frills but hold themselves exempt
From self-denial in the line of sex.
As press-ups are to health-fiends, genuflection
Is to the average Anglo-Catholic Prod.
What a good way to nourish one's erection.
God we hate Catholics and their Catholic God.

When Sister Flanagan from Houston Texas
Edited Baron Corvo for her Master's,
She changed the pronouns to reverse the sexes
As frills on chesterfields concealed their castors.
The text was passed unnoticed by the Syndics
And causes some confusion in the Bod.
Wait till she gets the Bible on the Index!
God we hate Catholics and their Catholic God.

A rugby-playing Catholic novelist,
Piers Paul Read, was lucky to be chosen
(Out of, we gather, a distinguished list)
To write about a new idea in frozen
Foods: when a rugby team crashed near Peru
On slopes the human toe had never trod
They ate each other. What a thing to do!
God – they ate Catholics and their Catholic God!

Michael Foley

CONVALESCENCE IN MAY

(After Laforgue)

It's early May. Lilac blossoms are out but I'm in
Tucked safely in bed with blankets up to my chin.

For a spoiled and frightened mammy's boy the sick room
Is heaven indeed – the nearest thing to the womb.

Extra pillows for sitting up, clean sheets smoothed out,
The rare fragrance of hot lemon drinks and fresh fruit

And the bouquet of magazines and paperbacks.
By the bedside Mansize Tissues in Handipaks.

With these I'll pull through although it was touch and go
And I've had a bad shock. A woman laid me low,

The most dangerous sort. You know these *faux naifs*
All modesty and jokes, hearts of flint underneath.

I'm not headyoumeecated she trilled *I'll never*
Be smart like you. Agreeing she wasn't clever

Was one of many games you had to play. *Counting*
The months she smirked on her best friend's *quiet* wedding,

Winking at me – for although the whole outlook was false
There was more pretence about sex than anything else.

O horrid teasing lady vile with daddy-love
Chasing you for pleasure, what was I thinking of?

Nightied or bikinied so coy on daddy's knee
Or bringing him in his Saturday morning tea.

All the thrills in innuendo and repartee
No touchy pretty girlie afterwards with me.

What chance had I? A brain of steel and flesh like silk
With the colour, richness and warmth of farm-fresh milk.

I was wiped – but I'll have revenge. Of all the priests
You've teased, the mod ones especially, one at least

Should call your bluff (and these days they do go too far)
Some progressive who'll pawn his acoustic guitar

And leave the Boys Club in the lurch to start anew
In the Motor Tax Office in Leeds, sticking you

In a one-roomed flat – which ought to be real enough
To crack your façade. Stick it in and break it off!

But – doctor's orders – I mustn't get worked up yet.
A few months' rest and perhaps I'll travel a bit

Finding the sea breeze a little too harsh but snug
Even so in my wheelchair and tartan rug . . .

Now my soft-boiled egg arrives and the lamps are lit.
An unusual convalescence, I'll admit!

Richard Freeman

UNDER THE HOSEPIPE

Not the purposeful beginning
Clamped to a shiny faucet,
The pipe stiffening from water pressure,
The glorious ending in a mythical rainbow
Woven into spray. That is not it. Life is
The dun loops where the lifted
Hosepipe lay, and how we con
Them for meaning: less the racetrack
Of wailing tyres, more a diagram
Of convulsions. More the result of a disembowelment
Than a rudimentary alphabet.
In place of a hidden, hope-bringing message,
Forgotten yardage, a path leading to craters,
Trenches, and the black, dug hyphen
Where the coffin comes to rest.
Under the hosepipe, no love.
In it, no breezes, no life. Nothing grows on it.
After it has passed the last drop,
The last tear, a worm enters the nozzle,
To fatten and stretch, to cast off
Eventually its rubber coat
And glistening, straited, suck at the tap.

John Fuller

ANNIE UPSIDE DOWN

What a position! I might as well be dead
    And suspended in the sea,
My feet treading the blue laid out beneath my head
    Like infinity.

I never thought the sky could press so hard
    Or rock needed my hair
As roots for the blood to pound through, with my feet starred
    Against the air.

It's the whole earth turned inside out like a sock
    And me just hanging on.
It's no more than a sixpenny magnet: give me a knock
    And I'd be gone!

Didn't they use to bury you upside down?
    I've felt like this in a cellar
Bending for coal. But then I wasn't snagged like a clown
    Or a wounded umbrella.

It's the wire that's got me as it pinches wool.
    Isn't there someone coming
Whistling up the mountain for sheep who could give me a pull?
    My head is drumming.

Once from bits on fence and thorn I wove a
    Skirt, something for free.
Retaliation! There never was a wall I couldn't get over:
    Now it's got me.

Where are Owl and Hugh, those gentle boys
    With deep pockets and a stone
For the dark pool in the wood where the eels made no noise
    Swimming alone?

How I ran after that pair just to be taught a
    Way to catch fish, and froze
As they held me by the bare heels with my hands in the slimy water,
    Tickling my toes!

Harry Tidy and Peter Shape would grin
    To see me on my head,
Who keep their balance as they keep their money in
    A feather bed.

And poor Tim Molehouse who for a whole spring
    Called to me from the garden
Might beg not for my finger for his mother's ring
    But for my pardon.

Why should he think it sinful not to marry?
    As if I belonged to him
One bit more than I belonged to Peter or Harry.
    Unhappy Tim!

There's many in their farms have shut their doors
    When I walked down the hill,
Though never did I once look back or without cause
    Wish them ill.

God help them with their sanctimonious drivel!
    They shall be stunned as an ox is
And shovelled into the black field under slabs that swivel
    Like pencil-boxes.

There let them gape as they have gaped from birth
    And gaping let them rot,
Each open mouth a rim of bone clogged up with earth
    Like a buried pot.

The soil shall not take me, caught up in my snare
    Like an old hanged ferret.
I am for the sun and the dissolving wind: the air
    Shall inherit.

I must weigh more than I thought. If I had wings
　　I wouldn't be in this mess,
Slumped in the sack of my body and gloomily thinking of things
　　To hate and confess.

Just like the redstart building I'd be gone
　　With a moment on the stone
To check my heartbeat and an eye for danger. One
　　Is too much alone.

Though pairs are rooted. Clumsy arms and legs
　　May be love's second-best,
And only wings brave gravity to lower eggs
　　Into the nest.

I saw the tell-tale twigs on precipices:
　　Amazing! But why therefore
Should *I* be fastened to the tilted hill with kisses
　　I did not care for?

I've had my arms round necks I saw too clearly
　　For any kind of rapture:
No passing longing for the ordinary is really
　　Worth the capture.

Rather avoid it. Single as the peak
　　Which every restless eye
Strays to when valleys are damp there's nothing that I seek
　　More than the sky.

Faces in rooms have too much of their own
　　Individual life,
Never the same when you look again, silently grown
　　Hard as a knife.

I've flown in dreams so perfect they'd convince
　　Me I might really try to
Waking, if only the old earth didn't say: 'Why, since
　　You've nowhere to fly to?'

I have no wings but only this dead skirt
    Peeled back like a glove
As once I had when I was young and nothing hurt
    So much as love.

The years fall out of your pockets, something comes in
    To your head like a passing thought
And can't be set to rights once it's got inside your skin.
    There: you're caught.

Hitched to the ribs of a field like so much mutton
    It's a wonder the crows don't come.
I might have thought of somehow trying to undo a button
    But my arms are numb.

Now I have had enough. It's all very well
    To hang here for a time.
At first I could have laughed: head over heels pell-mell
    Like a pantomime!

Let me be upright now and take a bow.
    Where's my fairy queen
To wave her wand and say that she understands just how
    Patient I've been?

Surely someone will come and fetch me and gather
    Me up and set me down
And all the escaped sheep will come running with their blather
    From their green town?

And the mountain will surely swing back in a while
    To point in the right direction
And I stagger about on the grass with a dizzy smile
    At my resurrection?

Surely the air after all this time has kept
    One secret however old?
I can almost hear it, and I would stay to hear it except
    I am very cold.

Just a whisper would do it, the wind among
    The branches where we stood
Once listening for the mouse's and the eel's tongue
    In the dark wood.

Or water falling as if for all time
    Out of the rock, so cool
And calm the silent threads seemed almost to climb
    From pool to pool

And the eye moving upwards to lose that downward sense
    And all the elements weave in
A strange stillness and mysterious excellence
    I could believe in.

Such a secret would be worth the wait
    As birdsong after a night
Of horrors. There's hope for things to happen, though too late.
    And they might. They might.

Roy Fuller

From MUSICAL OFFERING

1. COMPOSERS AND EXECUTANTS

Required: some daring emendation to life,
A real 'I think thee Ariel';
And thorough heroism and cosiness,
As in Debussy's ballet 'the wounded soldier
Is tended by the affectionate doll'.

The thirty-eight works for girl bassoonists
Studying in the musical orphanage:
What dedication to female youth, and art!
Moreover, the carroty composer, in celibate orders,
Must be absolved from ambiguous intent.

Actual smiles at Mimi's coughs and sobbing –
For the consummate reprise they punctuate –
Shakings benign of heads, as though the composer
Were not with Edward VII or the dead Infanta
But knew how the years approved his slowish tunes.

The western sky is pale as a complexion;
Passes like drying blood from red to dark.
Under the planets, long-legged spiders sleep
Close to earth. All species aspire to comfort –
'The wedding will be fun. Bears are good dancers.'

Evenings of playing Schumann rather badly
Must yield, as time moves on, to worse affairs –
The sparkling girlish mane next to a madman;
From filial love and intellectual accord
Depart the proud Oistrakh and Shostakovitch fathers.

Third-rate, one thinks, but truly meditative:
Perhaps as poets' Muzak it may live.

And then some harrowing melody comes out
Of the turning disc and half removes the doubt.

Besides, since youth, age or bizarre disaster
Tends somehow to confirm the rank of master,

Behind the notes one hears 1916 –
The fatal tin fish from the Boche submarine.

3. QUARTETS

'A willow or acacia over my brother's grave'
– Beethoven's epigraph for that *adagio*
Ceases to shock or puzzle (his brothers then alive!)
    As soon as we come to know

His elder brother had expired in infancy,
Relinquishing the name of Ludwig! Shakespearean
(As might have been prognosticated), the family
    Bed-life that formed the man.

Like all our worlds, mysterious but commonplace
Geniuses' worlds: how else could mortals contemplate
Quartets whose prolongations are designed to face
    With thanks the fangs of fate?

What different pain, nocturnal memories of things
Limping about the house we failed to see or bless,
From the great grief of varying keys and time that brings
    Mercy and happiness!

Robin Fulton

REMEMBERING A LETTER

Back from a long journey. Is skin-deep
the deepest that our furthest journeys reach?
You're far out in sleep. And I'm away
too, remembering a letter I sent you.
I left it in a mail box on an icy night –
it must have lost my hand's heat quickly.

Lewis Gardner

AT THE MAYTAG

Mrs Levine, don't be upset
by what you found in Sheryl's laundry.
She *did* bring it home for you to wash;
she's still your daughter.

True, she's a careless girl
and, true, one pair of men's underwear
would be easier to accept
than three of different sizes.

But think: you raised a girl with a big heart,
whose kindness extends to many.
And not just to love them, Mrs Levine,
but to keep them clean and nice.

Geoffrey Grigson

HELLAS

If I say I have come at last home
And here marble is warm
And these shrubs are pink by the
Coarser rocks and shake by the sea.

If I say I have come home
And here walls are whiter
Than paper and here at last I see
How red wine does apply to a sea.

If I say I have come back
To the starting and here
White high boats lay slow
Magnificent breasts on the sea –

I have to admit to me, like all
Other homes, this home-as-before
Cannot longer and as well
Warmly be home around me.

Madge Hales

PEACEFUL AND RIGHT

The holidays I had were lean.
At ten I saw the sea and got my
knickers wet paddling. We had gone
with the church outing.

So I have always envied people who
holiday all the time and can have
affairs with foreign places when they
want and fine lovers of different colours

waiting there in the sun specially for
them and eat smoked salmon every day
with vintage Möet and Chandon to tease
it down instead of making something

mundane tasty with original sauces
which becomes impossible eventually.
At home the farm was the holiday
but there is too much mulch and mud and muck

on farms for endless cleaning, so I always
envied those who had cushioned places
and paid others to keep the dirt down,
and had antiques and carpets

on the floors instead of tiles
and stone to scrub with thin
unrobust hands and a constant back.
And then again the tiles bright

red and blue were grey before the day
slacked. That was how the envy
started although the thin red hands
were my mother's and the noise

of doom in the household cough
was hers. I remember the sea
at ten was cold, and I wondered why
I was never peaceful and right.

Tony Harrison

GUAVA LIBRE

To Jane Fonda (Leningrad 1975)

Pickled Gold Coast clitoridectomies?
Labia minora in formaldehyde?
A rose pink death mask of a screen cult kiss,
Marilyn's mouth or vulva mummified?

Lips cropped off a poet. That's more like.
That's almost the sort of poet I think I am.
The lips of Orpheus fished up by a dyke
singing 'Women of Cuba Libre and Vietnam!'

The taste, though, taste! Ah that could only be

('Women! Women! O *abajo* men,
the thought of it's enough to make you come!')

the honeyed yoni of Eurydice

and I am Orpheus going down again –

thanks for the guavas soaked in Cuban rum.

Ian Harrow

NOVEL AS BIOGRAPHY

Page 77 turned down.
'The author of Moeurs . . . made the same judgements
On her character as we were later to make.'
A writer himself, or was it you?
Your battered now forgotten Durrell
Sent on with your stuff, returned
From Somewhere, USA, when you'd declined to
Follow his successor – and on the title page
The putting on and off of names,
The correction in your (slightly freer) hand
Above his original Christmas date and love (erased).

Francis Harvey

AT ARDS

All day the pheasants were honking
like vintage cars and
the cows cropped
young grass with a sound of
rending cloth. The ferns
were uncurling their croziers under
the candelabra of the chestnuts and
the hills were blue, blue as
the pools of bluebells in the grass. There was
a smell of crushed
almonds in the airs eddying
from the whins and
you were there with
a flower in your hand and I
was with you and I wanted
to take your other hand but
the children were there
as well and the cows.
I knew they would stare.

S. L. Henderson Smith

THE DIGNITARY

I was there when they brought you in
And had to certify you dead

For once you were serious and I could look
Into your eyes without the thought
You were always looking at someone else
Over my shoulder; the way your clothes hung loose
Dropping across the ambulance stretcher
Gave you simplicity, a natural poise
Like Juliet in her nightdress in the bedroom;
Death had accosted you with
"Madam Mayor, a final toast"

After so much hollow ritual
Of tinsel glitter, paper dignity,
Here was an honest sycophant
Laying his frosted finger-tips
Upon your ample purple lips

I would have kissed you had I dared.

Phoebe Hesketh

SECOND CHILDHOOD

Free as a thistle, white hair blowing,
he wanders through fields
leaving gates open as he leaves doors at home.
Without direction his days are slanted
by shadow and sun,
easy as a weathercock swinging
on the wind's heel.
Pulling sorrel seeds through finger and thumb
he scatters the coral beads,
tramples buttercups to gold-dust on his boots.

High time is harvest; a bronze moon
hangs over the hill;
by day the sun
ripens slowly as red fruit.
Wading through sand-coloured corn
he snatches the prawn-whiskered barley,
brings it home to play with all winter.

Happy, happy; this childhood is surer
than a child's,
unthreatened, outlasting life.
He will be a child all his days.

David Holbrook

ASHES

I am excited by a deep frost
That crusts the ground, that ferns
White fur on the cramped celery,
That crisps the mat of leaves.
We strip a fallen tree in the wood:
I build a fire, and tall flames
Shimmer pink and lilac in the air
(The paddock landscape boggles
Through the high licks of fire).
We tramp and tramp, dragging
Pine branches to the fire, gasping
Ice-cold air, our hands in pain,
Obsessed with the task, we saw
And axe the fibrous wood, trimming
Battlings and brattlings, stumps.
Soon, under a cold white moon
A white heap of ash trembles.
In my head I hear the 'Moonlight' interlude
From *Peter Grimes*: Britten is dead
Today, the white hoar marks his end,
The cold grip unrelieved all day
Death, and his death especially:
And on and on we tramped
Like the children in *Noyes Fludde*
Obsessionally clearing the wood,
Noting, even under the glinting rime
Evidence in spikes and buds
Of a new year beginning, even
As we brought this painful tangle
To a shining small mound of ashes,
The child and I, in our compulsion,
In our mixture of grief and joy,
Joy in being alive, in a dead frost.

Libby Houston

HARBOROUGH ROCKS

A man in breeches, steel and cords a bright skirt, picked out,
bridges, rope held by a thread, the flowering rain:
where we left off, and when, and which of us, pick up again

and where, low crags blocked off at the foot as well by bad light,
white: that we each were there then as thin spun as the thread,
anchor, if I had got the job, or not met you now dead

begin to run, like ants, uncovering, I put the stone back
to resurrect what pattern in black I presume, do not presume,
not I, on this date, bridging this little particular gloom –

brightness contained by grey, wet, a red apple lying in a drab
tangle for picking up, for how long, where we left off, ropes
coiled,
secured, to carry off: when I stood life on this rock it held.

Ted Hughes

NEFERTITI

Sits in the bar-corner – being bought
Halves by the shouting, giggling, market-tipsy
Farmers who squabble to pay –

She hunches, to deepen
Her giddy cleavage and hang properly
The surrealist shocking masterpiece
Of her make-up.

She can't breathe a word
That wouldn't short out
The trip-wire menace
Of her precariously-angled
Knees and wrist. Gorgeous, delicate,
Sipping insect,
With eyelids and lips
Machined to the millionth.

She gets her weird power
In the abattoir. All day you hear
The sheep wailing in religious terror,
The cattle collapsing to pour out
Their five gallons of blood onto concrete,
Pigs flinging their legs apart with screams

For the dividing steel
Of her pen in the office.

Ted Hughes

UNKNOWN WARRIOR

At curious eyes
He was conscripted

At sly fingers
He was equipped

At aimed perfume
He was armed

At bowel-churning glance
He received orders

At curl behind ear
He put on the helmet of dread

At sea-bottom mouth
He entered the trench and saw wounds

At lightly-disguised throat
He lay all night, on trembling earth

At sudden breasts
He went over the top

At wild thighs
He fell and rose again wet

At open belly
Battle-fury took his mind from him

At Mons
He found his monument

Brian Jones

THE SLAUGHTERHOUSE
FOREMAN'S SON

The slaughterhouse became the abattoir
when my promoted father took to suits
and no longer in the evening brought back home
that cold hollow smell of opened animals
or fingernails delicately rimmed with blood –
coincident with my entering grammar school
noosed in a black-and-silver tie and hobbled
with itching grey socks to the knee. On Sundays
we walked stiffly together in our new success
and have never since that time said what we thought.
I relate, however, to those departing cows
munching at mud as if it were lush pasture
in the paltry acre attached to the windowless
square building, towards which when it's time
they're led, nodding yes yes to their fate.

Jenny King

JOE

I went to your house once,
Up some stairs (was it a flat?)
With a number of boys, my brother's friends.
Three decades since.

Joe's birthday.
They sat on tables, drinking something fizzy –
What daring celebration! – while I hid
Out in the kitchen, trying to be busy.

But you came out – oh, I remember that! –
Rough-looking, humorous, and spoke gently,
And found me a still drink
And didn't blame me for being a girl.

Babies look over their fathers' arms in the park
And pass altogether into what they see.
The old slide into the foss of memory.
Between whiles, we must hold the two apart.

When I see bubbles rise in lemonade,
I sometimes think of feeling shy, afraid,
But sometimes watch them as a second hand
Constantly passing, like my prints in sand.

Lincoln Kirstein

DOUBLE DATE

Myself and Curtis Dean are seniors together, –
 half- and full-backs, junior-varsity teams.
Dean and I have fun, all sortsa weather
 sharing similar sexual dreams.

Curt and I do quite a lota double-dating,
 specially on Saturday nights, –
lotsa heavy-loving, (some x-rating),
 fanTAStic freeform farout delights.

Last Senior Prom he picks me up 7:30.
 We get Jane, – and friend (some unknown dame):
four of us, – crocked. Start talking-dirty,
 kick-off in the double-dating game.

First: breast-fondling. Then light n'lively kissing;
 next: pet-to-climax, (tongue & ear).
Then, partial-stripping. Still, something's missing.
 Jane plays the field; her friend's full o' fear.

Curt, – (he only ASKed her), – just suggesting shyly:
 'Stroke my pecker, please.' (Inside his pants.)
She gets sore: 'I'm a NICE girl!' (A lie.) She
 weeps; we'll miss that old high-school dance.

I laugh like hell, but Curt's bitched and bitter;
 starts up his car; gravel flies, wheels squeal.
Jane takes HER side. I sure coulda hit her.
 Curtis drives fast feeling one real heel.

We walk 'em to their door. They slamit, not speaking.
 Dean says: 'You drive. I'm too pissed to move.'
Must we go home yet? We stall there, seeking
 some real outlet for unrequited love.

95

Parked on a side-street for more serious-drinking
    Curt grins: 'I'm horny.' 'Beat-off,' I said. –
much the same we both of us were thinking;
    easier when formal-dress is shed.

Dumb simple hand-jobs aren't so all-fired thrilling.
    Dean sighs: 'I'll do you if you do me.'
Chances being caught queer can be chilling;
    we were jet-propelled on liberty.

Agreed on next steps albeit kinda risky;
    stripped bare-ass on that slippery back-seat.
Man o Man! That full-back's prime-time frisky!
    Mutual release is mor'n beating-meat.

But just like it was when those chicks got us started, –
    no chance for rocks-off. Fate interferes.
Headlights spot our tangle. We get us parted.
    Nudity unknots two bare-assed queers.

Flashlight glares hot on our raw frank condition:
    'What's goin' ON here?' inquires this Cop.
'Officer, we're drunk, sir.' Rank submission.
    Cop snaps: 'Curtis Dean! This gotta STOP!'

Yup. We're illegal. Policeman put it clearly:
    (he knows Dean's dad; acts paternally):
'Just pull your pants on,' proposing merely:
    'You're too drunk to drive, boys. Follow me.'

To Curt's house, bingo! Police-escort protection!
    Real motherly is Curt Dean's mother:
'You poor lambs look TIRED!' With no objection
    we bounce to bed. No further bother.

David Lan

BLUE PRINCE

1

Don Juan knees back the sheets, lies in the morning light,
  wipes down his cock.
Herr Faust reads final lines of verse, draws his blind tight
  and winds the clock.
Fresh breezes blow. Odysseus leaves his sailor's side.
  New sails unfurl.
The sun sips dry the rivulets Orpheus has cried
  for his lost girl.
Later they will fall as rain.

2

Stepmother Europe – true to type – plays cruel:
Offers paradigms (amo, amas) pre-
Tending scenarios now drilled in school
Weren't meant to blow her schools to buggery.

But if we clean from aged rebels cares and years,
  caked earth, dry foam,
And sharpen up their teeth, tongues, eyes, nails, knives and
                                                        spears
    and send them home
The present brood disown their dads. They shout abuse
  and lock their door.
Grandsons however love grandads – molars worn loose
  tough talk abhor.
They're placed on study walls again.
Later they will fall as rain.

3

Arth blunders in on Guin and Lance, chops off a pair
  of ears and balls.
Sunwards, trick flying Icarus draws loops in air
  and never falls.

Romeo buggers Juliet, dreaming he's got Benvolio
　　by the thighs.
Antigone gives up, sits down, lets warm tears flow
　　through tight shut eyes.
Rain clouds are forming in the skies.

James Laughlin

THE KIND

hearted Americans are
adopting Vietnamese

orphans it makes them
feel better about what

happened they did not
want what happened to

happen & did not think
things like that would

happen because so many
wise men told them they

couldn't if you had e-
nough liberty & napalm

and honor and airbombs
it's really sad about

the Americans the way
they're so kindhearted.

B. C. Leale

TO SAVOUR THE LAKE

To savour the lake the wait
-er winches the table down into it
& a chair & a bottle corked with
an esteemed vine-veined nose.
It is with a consummate ape
-like swagger glasses are frisked
for a lurking dust.
Sklug is everyone's sur-
name who draws lake-logged
corks. A lady's screams are cuddled
as a dead frog-leg steps oh o
-ver the rim of her
glass.

Laurence Lerner

GUARDI AT THE BALL

Swing from the ceiling   sink in the carpet
Bounce to the hangings   the ordered steps,
The wild surrenders   the sway and the gallop
The perfect repeatings   the moment of calm;

The Duke and his Duchess   the Doge and his Senate
The native the foreign   the clothed and the free
In lace and tiara   in lust and white velvet
In brilliants in laughter   all mortals all warm;

And I in a corner   in black and half-hidden
Cajoling a waiter   for truffles and wine,
Paid two hundred scudi   to snatch them from drowning
Preserve in its costume   the now and the here

To fend off the future   and leave on the canvas
The gold and the crimson   the flush of their flesh
No tear in the velvet   no word through the laughter
No black in my brush-strokes   no sound in the air,

Pamela Lewis

CHANGED HANDS

There are two men cleaning the windows,
it is a very long time since they were cleaned.
The man who lived here before us
was so rich he had no need to look out
to see his horizons.

He owned nearly a century when he died
and two acres, his two ungrateful children
looked unhappy as though it was a habit.
Older than us, they were covered in dust
they couldn't wait to shake off.

Both shook with neurosis, he stuttered,
she trembled and the housekeeper took pills,
tranquillisers to keep her hand steady
as she set the trays; she managed well enough.
She made a good cup of tea.

Now we run the house, by running upstairs
and downstairs, and by not meeting.
The servants who worked here wasted time
arguing demarcation lines and had never
read Parkinson, nor had the bosses.

I know because the gardener tells me so,
peeping between thorny scrawny roses.
I kneel on the other side of the bed;
if I stood up I would be weighed down
by fifty years of garden gleanings.

Madam has been dead for seven years, Master one,
and the dell is full of children making hay
while the summer lasts. It is now time
to look in and out of the windows of this house.
Soon it will be painted, the windows will wink.

Dinah Livingstone

THE SOFA

The smug bien-pensant
trendist social worker
condemns the slightly affluent
young working-class couple
for buying a two hundred pound sofa
or rather monster
three piece suite
in olive uncut moquette.
Wherefore was this waste
in such bad taste,
he cries, and you forget the poor?

I loathe the man's conceit.
I rage at his crassness.
For I know why I
have never spent more
than a pound or so on furniture.
My bones and blood
are at ease from centuries
of privilege and I can afford
shabbiness and eccentricity.

If I know, so should he,
that this young woman
(she works in a typing pool –
he disapproves of her more
because she is fashionable
from a chain store)
could be the first daughter
of sweated masses
bred in a crowded town,
whose loveliness at seventeen
will not vanish in her twenties,
that this young man,
also from our working classes,

perhaps correct and tightly buttoned,
by the rush of his wedding bewildered,
perhaps now looser and more geary,
but neither clever
nor well connected,
wants her to have comfort and luxury.
Why shouldn't they?

Know-all social worker,
you and your politics
are unfit to rule,
unless you have sympathy
from the inside
with every human body,
desiring the shock beauty
of your own and the other sex,
because that is natural,
feel fellow with the ugly,
respect the wishes of the people.

One day perhaps this couple
will make love on their settee
and laugh when it smells to heaven.
Perhaps their children
will bounce on it and their pleasure
will rate higher than furniture.
It will be scuffed with history
and then they may relax
and feel and be more free.

The Vanguard Party
which condemns uncut moquette
(because they would never want it)
is vile tyranny.

SIX DISENCHANTMENTS

The mirror you are
tells me too often
I am not beautiful.

The warm room you were once
was a good place to be.
Oh I'm no romantic –
catch me saying
'the walls of that room were warm fingers stroking' –
but it was clean and decent
I spent a long time in it, scribbling
and humming and rearranging at my leisure
the objects on the mantelshelf.

The rocket you are
still takes off occasionally
with a bump and a whoosh in the night.
Always
it's always the surprise of my life
and I have to hang on tight.

You say the scissors I am
are too keen on cutting.

You say
the teacher I am
is a terrible version
of a cartoon schoolma'am.
Too straightlipped & square shouldered,
pinstripes and pencil skirt –
strictly
too lewd to be true
and you can't be sure what punishment
she wants to exact from you.

So you thumb your nose and tell her
her boys will all grow up too soon.
Everybody gets to leave school
and throw his schoolcap over the moon.

God
the brickwall you are
these days – it doesn't
even crack when you smile.
Believe me I spent a lot of time
working with my fingernails at mortar **and lime**
before I started to so crassly bash
and batter my head at it, that brick wall.
Now even when I stop
it doesn't stop hurting at all.

CORNELIA

(after Propertius)

Keep heavy tears, Paullus, from my sepulchre,
Praying is not a key to the dark door.
Once ghosts pass beneath Hell's legislature
All roads are cul-de-sacs, bricked-in and blocked.
Though the god of the black house hear your prayer,
The shore that drinks your tears is a deaf shore.
Prayers move heaven only. Now Charon's fare
Is paid, the grave is overcast and locked.
The funeral trumpets meant this when my head
Was put above the blaze, and was melted.

Our marriage, Paullus, my family name,
All the assurances of motherhood –
What help were they to me? Destiny came
Without favours and reduced me to a load
Five fingers gather. In stagnant marshes
That enfold my feet, in prison darkness,
I am dead before my time, unjustly.
Deal gently, God, with what is left of me,
Or else, should my name in Hell's lottery
Turn up, and the judge condemn my ashes

(The Furies lingering, the courthouse hushed)
Let tantalising waters be achieved,
The wheels of torture stilled, the boulder heaved
Successfully away. Let Cerberus,
His lead and collar slack, hunt none of us.
Sentence me to catching water in a sieve
Should I plead falsely as my own advocate.
First, like one whom medals decorate
I claim descent from Africanus,
As those Carthaginian trophies demonstrate.

My mother's line is equally exalted –
Yes, titles bolster me on either side.
My girlhood clothes for Paullus were conceded
To the marriage torch, and like a mother's
My hair was tied, my life with his confused.
Soon to be divorced by death, I was his bride.
I am recorded on my headstone as his
Alone, and I call to witness ashes
Which you, Rome, should respect – my ancestors',
Beneath whose medals Africa lies bruised.

Because, forefathered by Achilles,
By Hercules who cracked whole palaces,
You, Perseus, took heart, please witness that
Paullus in his ordinance as magistrate
Never favoured me, nor by a single sin
To redden his fireside with embarrassment
Did Cornelia disgrace his name.
A model wife in his establishment,
She lived, unchangeable, beyond all blame,
Praiseworthily from marriage bed to coffin.

As part and parcel of my temperament
Came virtue – not through fear of punishment.
Whatever jurors sternly sentence me,
No woman sitting at my side will be
Ashamed – not Claudia, outstanding priestess
To Cybele of the towering head-dress,
Who tugged a boat to prove her chastity,
Nor Amelia, the Vestal Virgin,
Who produced, against a charge of carelessness,
Live cinders from her altar robes of linen.

Nor did I wrong Scribonia, my mother –
What else but death would she want changed in me?
Her tears are praise, and those of the city.
My bones are defended by Caesar's grief
Who mourned his worthy stepdaughter.
(We saw that tears come even to a god.)
My matron's uniform was warranted,
To no sterile house came death the thief.
You, my children, Lepidus and Paullus,
Comprise a comfort that is posthumous.

My last look was lodged with your affections.
Death snatched me on that gay occasion
When my brother was elected Consul.
My daughter, mirror of his Censorship,
See you follow my example and keep
To one man. So, children, with a lasting line
Pillar the home. This journey's bearable
If through descendants my actions keep their shine,
And when graveside praises prove impartial,
That is woman's wage – triumphant, final.

I commend our children, a common trust,
To you, Paullus. My cinders burn for this.
A father in a mother's role, you must
Shoulder responsibility for them.
When you kiss their tears, add my kisses.
The whole house begins to be your burden.
Don't let them see you weep, if you weep at all,
Deceive them, when they come, with tearless eyes.
Those nights of weariness when you recall
In sleep my image, Paullus, will suffice.

And when you talk to secret dreams of me,
Utter each word as though I might reply.
But should another love take pride of place
And camp discreetly in my bed, then praise
And tolerate my husband's wife, my sons.
I know that she'll surrender to your goodness.

Don't talk about me overmuch in case
She take offence at your comparisons.
Or should he rest content with memory,
Placing this high price upon my ashes,

Then try to feel for his advancing years,
Prevent the pain that is a widower's.
May the days death stole from me be yours,
Paullus take comfort from my sons when he
Is old. Thank God I never carried wreaths
For children who now carry them for me.
My pleading's done. Rise, witnesses and mourners,
While my reward is pondered by the earth.
May I reach heaven and my ancestors,
My bones conveyed there in the ship of death.

George MacBeth

THE OTHER WOMEN

I

And Haggar begat Mary, lice of the emerald season.
And Mary begat Verushka, gnu-thin.
And Verushka begat Elementa, who lay in the box-room,
     embedded mercy clinging to the envelope of perfection,
     without sheets.
And Elementa begat Silexis.

II

O Silexis, you were to blame.

III

And Silexis begat the others, walking small as mice or
     creepers between the interstices of the bedrock.
I see them coming.
And the others begat Haggar again in my dreams, huge as the
     arch of Constantine in the Roman Circus, legs working
     between the faces of granite or tile.
And the face of Haggar begat sandstone, that crumbled
     for mercy.
And Mercy begat Elementa, mate of the stooping thistle,
     long forgotten below the rafters the slippery spider
     dropped from.
And the rafters were broken, taken and cleaned.
As if they had never been, the very rafters were taken out
     and shaken clear of their last rustlings, paper and straw.
And Elementa begat the green penis, breeder of strawberries
     in the moulting wood-shed.
And the green penis begat Hope.
And Hope begat Silexis.

IV

Then came the day of the tiro, stropping razors through the
    mark of the sundered forum.

And all was well.

And the razors begat blood-shed, and the women who lay
    screeching *choke-me* hissed into flame.

And the flame burned.

And the flame burned for a long time.

V

Silexis.

And Silexis begat Anorexia, who ate only the fine grease of
    her own bowels, badger's meat.

And the crannies closed over the holes in the mind.

And the holes in the mind begat flame.

And the flame burned.

The flame is still burning.

Never to wake and hear them alone, screaming for
    attention in the work-basket.

Never to be a bitch, on heat for an isolated
    mentor.

Never to eat, and miss the smell of ammonia.

I used to dream of an island where all the men
    were chains you pulled in the shit-house.

And that was the end of it.

The very end.

Ah,
if only it was, if only it had been!

Roy McFadden

IMPOSTORS

1

Avuncular; clearly not
The diffident visitor,
Only a man disguised
In wig and robe to sell
Pink- and blue-wrapped toys.
Yet he was the harbinger,
Before the holly, the tree,
And the spires of carols astride
The indulgent City Hall.

2

Anachronistic; speech
Bogus Ascendancy,
Prejudice and power
Discreet in wig and gown:
For a child on Christmas Eve,
Caricatured in dream
His silhouette will loom
Like a rampant highwayman,
Arresting the harness bells.

Jean MacVean

DANCE OF MORGAN LE FAY

Two steps forward
and one step back.

The apple glows,
the apple glows
in the light
of the yellow rose.

Two steps forward
and one step back.

And rose and apple
turn to dust,
as they must,
as they must.

Two steps forward
and one step back.

I changed living men to stone,
my favourite lover is pure white bone.

Two steps forward
and one step back.

I sailed with a king
in a funeral ship.

Two steps forward
and trip, trip, trip.

I took his cold hand in my own.
Brother, I cried, where have you gone?

Brother, apple, rose and lover,
all are gone too far to recover.

Two steps forward
and one step back.

Apple I took from the wicked bough,
where, oh where, is your glowing now?

One step forward
and three steps back.

Wes Magee

THE BLACK SPOT

for Miranda

It lies on your satin cheek, an oval mole
no more than an ash smut, a minor blemish
    which doting Aunts call a beauty spot.

and for your two years it's been a passenger
growing as you grow, mostly ignored, swallowed
    up in creases when you laugh, but there!

For me it's the 'black spot', Blind Pew's calling card
which brought Billy Bones' gnarled heart to a dead stop;
    the trade mark of that groping old get

who tap-tapped his crabbed way into frightened lives.
Kisses won't erase it from your flesh, or love,
    and even now watching as you run

squealing through tall grass, innocent as sneezing,
I know its earth-print will be with you always
    down the long slope towards the dark, the dark.

Farida Majid

THE VISION OF A TEMPLE DANCER

Where he always is
he was in darkness,
with me, around
and inside, close,
very close.
I could feel him feeling.

Suddenly there was a window.
It had vertical bars.
It was a magic window.
No walls framed it.
No light came in
to line his shoulder
or face.
But I saw light outside.
I saw two faces.
Beautiful faces looking in.
Not silhouetted, well lit.
Jewels hung from
resplendent headdresses
above their frowned brows
and angry kohl-painted eyes.

One grabbed the bars
in fury.
She had long long
fingernails of gold.
A Chieng-mai dancer.
I heard their
ankle-bells jingle.

The darkness around
me dissolved
into night.
Over the lofty stone temple

the iron trident
trembled as lightning
streaked gathering clouds.
I lay naked in the courtyard,
hands above my head
in 'pataka' mudra,
knees bent apart
in 'plié'.

Heard ankle-bells again,
approaching.
They seized me
by each wrist
fingernails digging in.
Dragged towards
the river, I felt
grass and grit, night-wet,
screech past my back.

The temple-ghat
I know so well.
They stopped
on the topmost step.
I rolled my head
from side to side,
the two guardian lions
carved in dust-pink
stone did not turn
to look or greet,
just stared into air
above the river.

I did not see what
it was that one of them
pulled out of her
gold embroidered girdle,
she was so swift.
The instant I caught
the metallic gleam
in her moving hand
there was the impact.

My body was cleaved
limb by limb,
breast by breast.
As each piece came
apart they picked
it up, flung
it in the water.

In the water
each turned into
a lotus, luminous,
gliding on its own
reflection on dark
ripples disappearing into
darkness where he was.
Where he always is.

Derwent May

A FEBRUARY MEMORY

The black ducks were riding out on the wind-waves
That February morning; still I could see
That the water darts pooling on their backs,
The wind falling like branches from a tree,
Did nothing to dispel the black ennui
With which they waited for the time to pair.
So I shouted and clapped the hollows of my hands
And with gratitude they sprang on to the air.

The Djakarta girl who cooked for me every day
Looked like those birds: she squatted on the floor,
Eyes dull as the water in a pail,
Mouth lying flat on her rounded jaw,
While across the kitchen the sun, yellow and raw,
Slotted through the banana trees in a rain –
Till I called for the sweet, jungle-spotted tea
And at the sound she sprang into smiles again.

On Monte Carlo station one afternoon,
My father told me, he saw a sleepy man
Waiting to take his ticket. When he got there
His ticket was levered up by a bulgy hand
And corresponding left-hand fingers began
To tear off the outward portion. They got half-way,
Then stopped. And the bulgy hand fell forward again
With the flapping ticket left for the Last Day.

But I distract myself with my father's story.
Indolence is not ennui; and this afternoon
I am like the birds and that girl, not the ticket-collector:
Much travelled in mind and body, sitting down in a room
In Warsaw, now; some men on the roof with broom
And iron spikes breaking the frozen snow.
It shuffles to the gutter, and icicles glint
Dropping with it down to the courtyard below.

A boy shouts down there; the snow thuds.
Alone, without desires, my mind goes back
To the boy I was fifteen years ago,
Slipping through rhododendrons down to a lake,
Listening whether the wind carried a quack;
The bored birds out on the water's bare
Shining surface; and when I clapped my hands
How with gratitude they leaped on to the air!

Gerda Mayer

SAGE

If you are slightly bored, you are in luck,
and should not ask the gods to organize
too long an outing from the days you dwell in;
such prayers have a knack of being heard,
and exile is a hard land to do well in.

The guru spoke – and from experience!
And yawned. And wished himself ten bolts of thunder hence.

Roger Mitchell

HOMAGE TO BEATRIX POTTER

I

I do not know a lot about Beatrix Potter,
but if she were my daughter,
I would tell her not to bother, so much,
about good behaviour.

I would wonder what I had done to her
and under what pretext
to have been turned into a Macgregor
for her Peter to anger.

And in a garden, over an issue like property.
And in the company of imploring
but otherwise quite useless sparrows.
Life was difficult in the nineteenth century.

But I don't think mothers, even then,
sent their sons to the usual slaughter
with a chuck under the chin
and a wry word about potted father.

And then went out to buy five currant buns,
including one for their errant son,
who might or might not, according to the whim
of dread, come home again.

I think of the mouse with her mouth full of pea
who stopped to gag something kind
but incomprehensible, and the cat
who twitched at the bright orange fish in the pond.

And the hob-nailed boot that kicked
through the potted plants, and the raised rake,
and the tiny rage at the little rabbit
whose only habit was eating.

I wonder if minding mother would ever matter
in a world of Macgregors, and others,
who like to see some things grow,
but not others.

II

I am the father of Peter Rabbit.
I was eaten by Mr and Mrs Macgregor on Sunday
after being skinned in the tool shed,
boned in the kitchen,
and boiled for several hours in a metal pot.
Mr Macgregor said I was good.
Mrs Macgregor wasn't sure,
thought I was a bit stringy in places.
I was caught in the French beans,
a rake point driven through my skull.
I lived to be an example to my son.

III

It was the drawings I remember most,
the careful cabbages and a radish
that Peter seemed to pick his teeth with,
the tiny slipper in the dirt, and always
everything about to melt into the page
like snow fallen on clear water, two versions
of the same thing merging, a bright inhuman
whiteness, a small world paling into it,
like animals pretending to be people,
an invisible barrier disappearing,
an unimaginable brotherhood
of living things, as a book stands between
nothing and the person reading it.

John Mole

BESTIAL HOMILIES

Darwin's Ape weeps underneath a tree –
Further, my God, than ever and ever from Thee.

Lear's Owl is singing to his small guitar –
Love is a pussy. What beautiful pussies there are.

Carroll's White Rabbit hasn't made it yet –
He drops in at the lab. for one last cigarette.

Tennyson's Eagle plummeting from his crag –
The world belongs now to the cormorant and shag.

Melville's Whale, a transatlantic freak –
Out of the mouths of babes . . . and even dolphins speak.

Somebody's faithful dog, no matter whose –
Good dogs are always faithful. Treacherous ones make news.

My cat purrs loudly through the bulletins –
Her aerial whiskers twitch, indifferent to our sins.

Behold, a tiny autocratic mouse –
He's thinking big. He plans to overthrow the house.

Be warned by Nature not to let things go –
The animals prepare to say: We told you so.

Abigail Mozley

THE SUMMER I TAUGHT ENGLISH
TO THE FRENCH

the summer I taught English to the French
it was hot and blue
the house was full of defeated flowers
abortion posters
and the plaster waltzers
Walt Disney dancers, curves of green and gold
chipped plaster
the perfect sadness of an odeon romance
and my head was a language tank
words under glass
like fishes

I got interested in jukeboxes and photography
demonstrated for abortion on demand
I carried on teaching English to the French
'Excuse me but I seem to have overwound your cuckoo clock.'
'Don't worry I never did like that cuckoo clock anyway.'
it was hot and blue
and dying flowers miscarried red petals
all over the dusty house
a rank smell of dead nasturtiums and geraniums
I studied the situational dialogues
and photographed the plaster statuette
from sixteen different angles
caught their Palais glide
against lace curtains, concrete, roses, long grass, lettuces
an obsessive succession of passionate swoons
quel trucage

the trouble with love is the language
such heavy duty Anglo-Saxon stuff
like those trees outside
heaving, restless as women
shifting their silks, their skirts,
too much
kitsch et charmant, c'est mon style
I like it danced on ice
to Wurlitzer or Mills or AMI
ami, cheri

ah me it was always hot and blue as a movie
and I was always teaching English to the French
'Excuse me but I seem to have damaged your plastic flowers.'
'Don't worry I never did like those plastic flowers anyway.'
so hot and blue the beach was stopped by it
laid out flat
even the people silenced by it, diminished by the heat
a real french navy hello sailor afternoon

I was thrown, I was blown
by his Billy Budd looks and his matelot top
by his thighs and his bleu de ciel eyes
and I thought I would blow it
sink toute la boutique
in his sailor blue, movie blue, navy blue thighs and his eyes
have a whale of a time
short as a postcard
I blew it
washed him down with soda water

he left at 8 a.m.
looking tired, a denim blue fatigue
I put on my glasses and my soft black dress
and went on teaching English to the French
'Excuse me but I seem to have broken your Skegness
souvenir ashtray, lost your Robin Hood hat, run over
that plastic gnome outside and also the cat.'
'Don't worry I never did' etcetera
we all laughed and the blackboard rattled

but then he started sending
indecipherable messages
morse code poems
to do with the sea and trees
and referring to some disaster I didn't recall
some accident
he felt he must redress
in verse
I was depressed

I like it danced on ice
I didn't reply
I carried on teaching English to the French
apologies, small ruptures, ballroom fractures
distressed the blackboard
the chalk dust settling like fall-out
on my soft black frock
I continued to admire the plaster waltzers
for their chipped and plastered style
the only injury I could uncover
was a soft bruise
gently bluing the skin, no blood
and it continued hot
the house full of red defeated flowers
abortion posters
plaster statuettes

Angus Nicolson

BUDS

butterfly fluttering at the window   that
is cause for distraction from
multiplication two
times one is two it cant escape
attention of the class times
two is four and   she in the second
row her eyes alone are
on the book   my eyes on
her   high cheekbone gathers in
the light the smoothness
of her skin
            then teacher snaps
us from our spell and she
in the second row is first to raise
her O so lovely head   next lesson

a for apple b for
bargain with the devil c for
care   she doesnt care & d for
doesnt even
know

Jeff Nuttall

SECOND DEPARTURE

The lovers danced their locked loins,
Working the purchase of groin's leverage,

Turned their gyrations to a winced speed
Til time could interbreed with sperm.

The lady-girl extracted life-gouts out
And turned about their dreaming.

Their clenched selves spin down a chimney of ages
That leaves them spent when the spasm's rage is quenched.

They lie on a beach, on a white sand moon.
Oars creak. She's soon to go.

'Come away now,' the kinsman booms
To the girl-child whose woman womb drained the heart
　　out of me.

We whirled into our muscular vortex, slow-motion cyclone.
Anticipation of my starspurt by her chrysaloid flowering
Split climax, superseded the transcendent apex
By superimposing, a tenth of a second early,
Superior access to eternity. Skinned of self,
Wrenched out of contingencies, woke eye to eye wondering
　　our whereabouts,
Our bed impossible to place because 'place' wasn't our
　　situation.

The lake, secret-set,
And eyeglass dropped in,
Studded, clear as trapped sky, in
The dryshaved moors over Pateley.

The drowning plethora of rhododendron.
The silent invocation of water
So still it survived a century or more,
Defeated change.

And she, languid from love,
Laid with the lees of love fawn-fingering
Aflow along her fallow thigh,
Stood by me in memory clad differently.

In white, in young clothes, lace.
My sister, intimate from infants' liaisons.
The impermissible honey still viscous
On my eleven-years' fine-bred fingers.

We come our minds clear of time because our vows were
                                                  made
Two centuries before, incestuously.
We land on the crescent of love's crystalline coast
To find the relatives present, the kinsman,
His great plumed hat; our father waiting silently
In the stern of the dipping bark
Out deep in the fret of the future. Now we both go.

Sean O'Huigin

ARAN POEMS

dog
by the
sea side
dead dog
sea dog
fangs by
the tide bared
sea dog
lying
red skin is
skull tight
hole in
his red side
poor dog
the sea dog
gone the next
day

like some
prehistoric
caterpillar
the spine of
a great whale
lay upon the
seaweed
on the shore
upon the rocks

blues &
purples &
whites &
yellows &
pinks &
greens
three wrens in
a thorn bush
ceaseless
aran wind

Frank Ormsby

WAITING FOR A CONNECTION

No room for flux, it seemed, on platform three,
So bare the benches, noticeboards so clear,
And only the simplest signs for company:
Tickets and *Waiting Room* and *Gents*; less near
Lamps and *Inspector* broadly facing me.

I did not see the hanging station clock
Record the minute when your head appeared
Above the footbridge railing, or your frock
Against the signal-box. You must have neared
Thinking me distant, where I gauged the lock

Of rail on sleeper. Then my idle eye
Detected you, a toe's breadth from the stone
Edge of the platform. From that minute I
Could not remember how it was alone,
Waiting untroubled there, directed by

Plain lettering. And even then to right
And left of me, *Way Out* the clearest signs
Insisted and a kindly morning light
Detected oil-stains where the shining lines
Stretched out their promise. But your eye was bright,

The bland front-carriage nosing into sight.

Rosie Orr

(HOW VERY GREAT IT WAS
TO SEE YOU AT ALL)

the poet sits elegantly
in his leather chair
he has polished his boots
he wears new underclothes

modestly
he hands little slices of himself
around the room
the audience admires cross-sections of the intestine
(it is stuffed with sausages and holy oils)
and politely examines the rectum
(it is full of sequins
and old newspaper cuttings)

the poet's jacket is fully lined
with little magnifying mirrors
during the applause he unbuttons it
and smiles proudly at himself

Trevor Pallister

THE RAMPTON POEMS

Together we struggle to the M1
and you remark on the shit.

An open skinny footbridge spans a space,
goes nowhere. Someone's had a factory smashed.

'My father worked there 30 years.'
Engines for India, bombs for H.M.G.

Such fragile products and now itself,
its space, price tagged by a London broker.

Head out now in great circles. Leeds
drains off left, the salt road shines.

In the glovebox, the Rampton poems.
Furtive from birth, their smell reminds of nests,

One said 'Dawn follows the emeralds
of night forming stars.'

And another:
'Fire and ice consume each other.'

We go on, rising, falling,
easy driving on the dry white road.

'All assertions are drivel,' you said.
At exit 35, the tar works' molecular smell.

My children were born in Sheffield.
You snore, the road is diamond white.

Nottingham, asylum county.
Rampton, Saxondale, New Balderton.

'It was a dark and stormy night, Jake told a story
'It was a dark and stormy night, Jake . . .

You joke and the traffic hoards immense
inertia as the night falls.

The poems go stale in the glovebox.
Romford, deep in rubbish, dismantles its market.

There Brownjohn will read, not quite conversation,
poetry not quite like the Jake joke.

We will pass twice through Nottingham,
the poems fermenting in their secrecy.

'The green brown blending land
holds crimson glowing chariots.'

Poetry travelling North,
reflections travelling South.

'Dear Dr Noble,
   'I must . . .' The perfect intent, on grubby paper.

Brian Louis Pearce

THE TELEPHONE IN THE DESERT

The telephone, springing up
   like a black snake
   in the dune field,
open and yellow
   the sand
   in its desertedness,
the motor-bike in the upper room,
   the tailor's dummy
   in the market square,
outside the church, an easel; the statue
   outside the town hall,

the inclination of the shadows
   like a temptation
   in the wilderness,
like a knife in the mind, or a sword
   prepared for your own heart also,
   each is the juxtaposition
of the infinite with the finite,
   the one
   with all:
an action, a word, a look, in which the entire world
   is screwed up into a ball

or a few cubes, an arrangement
   of lines on paper,
   a thought, a word,
a note at the highest pitch
   of the violin
   or the oboe's rapt
accompaniment of the human thought and word:
   this, in a word, is the world,
   the world in its wholeness, a world
of endless and infinite meaning, wrapped
   in fact, in the Word.

Peter Porter

SHORT MAD POEMS

This is not madness in its fashionable shape,
But wrong parts for the failed machine,
Glucose afternoons when cancer comes.
Mad is a truth not applicable –
Come here and I'll comfort you
Though there's no comfort in the world.

Preludes, theorems, gestures,
Words written after sudden waking,
The Dissenting Spirit's Song Book.
Now will you buy your lyrics here?
A few poems to show for the agony
Which would have happened anyway –
Skilful exploitation of fat chance.

At five o'clock
I won't switch on the light.
It belongs to work and hope
And I want to see
Ineradicable dark.

It would cost a fortune
To change the façade across the square.
Words are cheaper,
Poems very good value,
So let me talk to you about style.

On to the fifth poem and nothing mad yet.
'For flowers can see, and Pope's carnations
knew him.' Whether that is mad or not
Has nothing to do with whether it is true,
And whether it is true doesn't affect
The power of its poetry.

To Dr Tarr and Professor Feathers'
To talk about myself –
You go up and your partner goes down,
It's a syphoning and you're
Selfishly disturbed. Home with just
One definition: paranoia is the name
Given to the soul's atmosphere.

At the cinema,
Ken Kesey's loonies and their nurse –
Among all the simplifications
And half-truths one unsentimental insight:
The custodians of the mad
Need their patients' afflictions
To stay sane themselves –
And that applies to you, Dr Big Bad Wolf,
With your hollyhocks in Parsifal Road
And your memories of the Ringstrasse.

Loving reason is a form of madness.
Like this: go along with the warped definition,
See angels round the wash basin,
Enter the auditoria of self.
No, you insist on seeing reality,
On farming your mind in the working world.
Isn't it mad to resist comfort
And find eloquent evidence of despair?
Stephen Crane's creature devouring
Its own heart – such a little book
And so thorough a homecoming.

Words, pictures, carvings, notes –
All annotations, nothing real.
Never, never, never, never, never.
Five trochees in a row: other shreds of words
Around admittedly, but can your critic
Or psychiatrist find the seat of pain?

If Lear or Dostoyevsky came to my front door
I'd close it in their faces. Haven't I
A sanctum of my own with horror in it?
Helen beside the tomb of Proteus,
Praying for help and help does come –
The sky opens and the audience goes home.

The death worm crawled from Enkidu's nose
And at last Gilgamesh was convinced.
As hero, he was spared the fate
Of living with the walking dead.

Two thirds of the human race
Is younger than me. My children have begun
To catalogue my eccentricities.
Ten years from now I shall say to them,
'I'm alright. But it's madness to be old.'

W. Price Turner

A SEAGULL CONSIDERS THE POETS

('*I hate seagulls*' – *Iain Crichton Smith*)

They sit on bollards and stare
out to sea. They carry the air
of superior beings, yet seem
unable to rise from the ground.
I scream over their pink faces
but the papers they flap away
never contain any bread.
Often found in quiet places
contemplating the stone dead,
they sometimes stoop to inspect
tiny shells long since dispossessed
of any blob or spasm. Best
to ignore them, else they elect
themselves ocean laureates
and unroll interminable scrolls
of bombast, flecked incantations
only they can understand.
As I scan panic stanzas wriggled
into sand, my shadow undulates
across their lumpish elongations:
odd birds, dribbling bedraggled
extravaganzas of rage or loss,
all bled on the page from one hand.
They look starved. Let them eat words.

Craig Raine

AN ENQUIRY INTO TWO INCHES OF IVORY

We live in the great indoors:
the vacuum cleaner grazes
over the carpet, lowing,
its udder a swollen wobble . . .

At night, the switches stare
from every wall like flat-faced
barn-owls, and light ripens
the electric pear.

Esse is percipi – Berkeley knew
the gentle irony of objects, how
they told amusing lies and drew laughter,
if only we believed our eyes.

Daily things. Objects
in the museum of ordinary art.
Two armless Lilliputian queens
preside, watching a giant bathe.
He catches the slippery cubist fish
with perfumed eggs. Another
is a yogi on the scrubbing brush.
Water painlessly breaks his bent
Picasso legs.

Clothes queue up in the wardrobe,
an echo to the eye, or a jangle of Euclid.
The wall-phone wears a pince-nez
even in the dark – the flex
is Jewish orthodox.

Day begins.
The milkman delivers
penguins with their chinking atonal fuss.
Cups commemorate the War
of Jenkins' Ear.
Without thinking, the giant
puts a kettle on the octopus.

Peter Reading

CAMPING PROVENÇAL

Camping Provençal. Notices: (1)
Tourists may only settle in the camp,
after if having checked in at the office
they know their places. (2) The campers' dresses
must be correct in camp. (3) Please no noise
between the 22 and seven-o-clock.
(4) In the camp, parents must watch across
their children. (5) Take care of the plantations,
don't set up nails nor pour dish-water on
the trees. (6) Fire-woods are forbidden. (7)
Linen must dry discreetly. (8) Detritus,
put this into the dustbins. (9) Showers-bath,
wash-house and W.C. must be kept clean.
Water is quite uncommon in Provence.
(10) Management is NOT responsible
for thefts. (11) Speed don't exceed 5.
(12) *That* box is reserved alone for throw
sanitary-towels and periodicals.
(13) These rules must be respected under
penalty of your time expiring here.

Peter Redgrove

HORSES OF THE DUST

Ants like slim horses trotting in their valleys
Galloping with hollow hooves over the grey cinders,
Caught in a shower darkening in splodges
They are faster than the rain, they see it coming
Like the hulls of glass liners. Ants full of grass,
Their lips pincing grass-tufts, their tight plates
Panelled over juicy flow, ant-milk
Oozing from their leg-joints; and parched ants
Like lacquered skeletons with ruminant jaws.
They live in a city which is called The Queens.
Each room in that city is called A Queen.
Sometimes their Goddesses are carved within tree-trunks,
Others are flat Goddesses, spreading under stones;
Lift one, look into the Goddess's side, watch her blood
In its rooms, each blood-speck a skeleton,
Or a thin horse, exquisitely formed.

Harriet Rose

IN PAMIERS 1325

She wore a white dress
when they marched her to the village square
when she was a pillar of shot stars
and the fire slid
up the smooth side of her bare leg
her eyes fixed on Fournier.
And there was consolation
in the crossed arms above her head
and in the words wrenched
from the hot pyre of her bowels
at the Aparelhamentum – public confession.
And her dress burst into flame sheets
billowed like the tent
at the world's roof
where skies close.
Truths like the parched ground
of a dog day
cracked at the hill's edge.
And green willow flexes
in her green eyes.
blood crusts black
where they removed her nails.
blood black over blacked skin.
And the crowd's din
was hushed in expectation.
She has magicked the flames cold
And she is frozen.
And every demon is a day of her past lives
And the flame deluge has tuned into the future
words flexing fire.
Electrons beeping numbers
shoot like stars
merge in the green eye of God.
A silhouette of silver lightning
crosses under the shadow
where she moves.

Carol Rumens

SYLVIA PLATH: A DRAMATIC MONOLOGUE

Scatter my words to Atlantis
or the chill-lipped mills of the sea;
I am full as the Taxcan mountains,
for the earth has married me.

Old patriarch dressed in marble,
I've hung your beard on a vine,
and thrown your frown to the leopards of sun
that are leashed to my wrist, that are mine.

I've dropped a gleam of water
like a rock, and like a tree
two heavy, bright-skinned children
for the earth has opened me.

Blue-stockings with black notebooks
are howling jealousy,
the Sybil chokes on her cobwebs
for the earth has aproned me.

Old patriarch dressed in marble,
why does your eye spark still
under the frown of the earth-haired man
who calls my leopards to heel?

His traps are as sweet as brambles
and old as the hills of the sea,
and the wound is deep and perfect
where the earth has married me.

Vernon Scannell

VIEW FROM AN ELECTRIC CHAIR

Steel bangles clamp wrists,
Head half-nelsoned by a cold arm,
Feet fastened firm,
Buttocks clenched like fists,
I am not comfortable
But I do not complain;
I would be agreeable
To sit here for a long time,
But I know – I almost know –
In seconds I must go.
The bald wall blurs, grows hair;
Voices in the gallery
Melt to a running slur.
Soon I shall be an unpleasant memory,
A jockey of nightmare.
Wedged between my thighs
My sex is shrivelled to a wince,
Could cause now little offence.
And what would that girl with unhappy eyes,
Mooning at the music's edge,
What would she think to see me now?
All I wanted was to make her glad,
Pity was all I felt for her.
I wanted to make her smile and I did
When we went outside in the glittering cold,
She was happy, I swear she was –
Happy until the stars went out
And I grew huge
Loud bugler of the winter night
Heard through drowning thunder.
I did not want to hurt her,
The music was too loud.
And now my sex is shrivelled
As all of me will be
When the hand, a pale blind rapist

Moves to the lever
To grasp and throw it down.
I will sit the dance out
As the light in the cell block dims
And the orchestra of mugs and spoons begins.

Susan Schaeffer

DELUSION: 16

My spine is golden, old Russian gold.
My spine is made of gold, every inch of it,
Every link.
It has taken some time to arrange this:
It was very important.

My head is set on the top held by the prongs
Of the neck. My head is a diamond,
The nails and nipples are jewels,
The belly button, etc., engravings.
If I curl myself up, I turn into a ring.

If I coil myself around you, you are caught
And cut off. Immediately, a canopy springs up
Over your head, an umbrella of spines.
Immediately, witnesses and priests grow out of the floor
Like terrible vines. If you move,

They sway in toward you. Already
You can hear the sacred words gathering in the room
Like smoke. Something is burning.
The ring itself is red as fire.
It is singeing your clothes.

The smoke is getting thicker and thicker.
There are cries of *fire*, alarms.
The whole building is leaping with old gold,
With red gold. Floors are falling.
I won't let go. You are fluted and beautiful

And white like a scallop. You are so beautiful
I embrace you with all my arms.
Finally, you tire, your muscle lets go,
You open your shell. My stomach takes you in.
My arms melt back in.

The helmeted man finds me.
He holds me up to the light; he is sly.
He slips me into his pocket.
He is going to take me home to his wife.

Penelope Shuttle

BIRTHDAY OF AN UNHAPPY
WOMAN

Her birthday falls on the full moon.
Her despairs crack,
like eggs broken against a window.
Her daughters dance in their brightly-stitched bones,
particles of moon constantly changing their courses.

Her hive of dreams is invaded by children.
Their feathery squeals reach the sky.
They are child-ghosts whirling lassoes.
She ladles honey into their giggling mouths.

She walks in the dark garden.
The moon, unappeased, remains in cloud.
The woman's steps are moon-steps.
She is aware of the craters in the lawn.
The black butterflies of night brush her face.
She waits.
The garden is cold, desolate, unfestive.

When the moon emerges from clouds,
it lures her to the edge of the lilacs.
The tumult of moon streaks the sky green-grey.
The moon looks like a bit of bric-à-brac, she thinks.

But the moon resounds in her.
She recalls her own eclipses and orbits.
She knows she is no stranger to the moon.

The lumps in her breasts belong to the moon.

James Simmons

KNOCKING ON

The more I wear glasses
the less well I see.
Mary at the study door
was hazy to me,

hard on eyes to look at,
hard on mind to grasp.
I panicked and slammed on
my spectacles fast

and lost her, rightly,
for glasses are grotesque,
like the ache in my elbows,
the pains in my breast.

Love is for the young ones.
Even if they're not
elegant or gentle
their blood runs hot.

After experience
we measure our resource,
the pulse beats softer
further from the source.

Intricate and careful,
too fond of style,
even the nicest girls
turn away to smile.

Cuchulain at his last post,
Sweeney in the trees,
hands out of plackets
and off plump knees:

I should seek, with those men,
the danger and the wet.
Pull back the sheet, love,
soon, but not yet.

C. H. Sisson

THE ZODIAC

And so, we need divide the year;
Also, the human character.
Aries at first, Aries the Ram,
Whose neighbour in the sphere I am:
Taurus who, lowing for Europa,
Must be content with grass for supper;
The other neighbour being Gemini,
Though two might be thought two too many.
Cancer crabs everyone in sight
And therefore has the shortest night,
While Leo tries to be benign
In spite of his ferocious sign.
Virgo, we all know, cannot last
Even until the summer's past;
Her, Libra seeks to equalise
With equal balances of lies,
Though Scorpio would bite the tail
Of any too ambitious male,
And Sagittarius shoot arrows
At aeroplanes, and bring down sparrows.
Capricorn is a goat, and cannot
Conduct himself as if he were not;
Aquarius, with watery eye,
Does nothing else but cry, cry, cry;
Pisces, however, swims in tears
Till harmless Aries re-appears.

Why quarter and divide in three?
Too much brilliant astronomy:
The heavens would not stay still, and grew
Quickly to circle out of true,
Till all the scholars, from their book,
Knew that the sky must be mistook.
Then came a learned supposition
That the erroneous position

Taken up by the wandering stars
Must reflect on the characters,
Not of astronomers and pedants,
But all the new-born innocents
Who had not yet twisted their minds
Into the pattern of mankind.
In case the constellations faltered,
Science would see that they were altered:
So, anything you care to hope
Is enlarged in your horoscope;
Whatever makes you shake with terror
Is grimmer in the written error.

If Aries only were a ram,
And Gemini, twins in a pram;
Taurus, among the cows, and Cancer
Not so much favoured as the lobster;
If Leo kept his woolly head
Inside his cage, and Virgo's bed
Were no more visited than most;
If Libra weighed up pounds of tea
And Scorpio died of D.D.T.,
Who'd be afraid of Sagittarius?
Or find no life-belt in Aquarius?
If Capricorn were only goat,
The fear of butts would be remote,
And indeed, but for scholarship,
Pisces might end as fish and chips.

BLACKHEADS

Now in the after play
I press my fingers against
these blemishes on your
warm and beautiful back
— these little, worm-like, fatty
masses in your follicles —
where I have just held your flesh
in the grip of passion.

What are they made of? They leap
forth, the black tips followed
by the sinuous tails like
miniature streams of toothpaste
but a sickly white.

Can dirt be so white? Are they made
of soap? Who would dare
analyze them for taste?
Though I have run my tongue
lovingly over your body,
I would lack such courage.

Some are so deep they take
seconds to empty, if
indeed they do empty.
Has no one squeezed them before me?
Were they there all the time,
gathering, deepening,
waiting for the touch of my fingers,
secret imperfections
kept virginal for a lover?

Julian Symons

CENTRAL PARK

A walk in Central Park,
New York friends tell me, is far from being a lark.
If lucky enough to escape attack by muggers
You will attract the more insidious attentions of buggers.
At night it is even more dangerous than the subways,
Those hubways
Of delinquency and violence.
                                    But I walked there at dusk
And felt as safe as if I were in the office of Dean Rusk.
It is a city park, hard cracked and bare
And melancholy, like the brown bear
Who paws at his cage in the Zoo. In places the grass
Looks as if it has received attention from (to quote Cummings)
                                    Lil's white arse.
The lamps are wired over to prevent their destruction
And boys playing baseball are warned: 'Instruction,
Use soft ball only.' The cars move through it, spat out by the
    great suction
Cleaner on West, sucked in again on East. Trees, greenness are
    incidental,
For this park is part of the roaring mental
Delirium of the city. Although the prospects please
The park is a place of excitement, not ease.
It is this, and not the assaults of sluggers and huggers
That make a walk in Central Park,
In daylight or after dark,
Something short of a lark.

HARVARD

Harvard, Cambridge, Mass.

A fine spring day. On the Charles River boats pass

Under the bridges, urged by the earnest doing their best to
  fulfil

The exhortation (Nicholas Longworth Anderson Bridge) that
  they should develop their manhood in the service of the
  nation's will.

Across the river the Business School, and behind

Me colleges and hamburger houses mixed up, a little red brick
  Georgian and a lot of fake, resigned

To the contiguity of modern blocks where the students like to
  live.

Watching their casual ease, eagerness, brashness, which derive

From the democratic process, I wonder how much will survive

Of all this as America feels its power

Growing. We are formed by our institutions, they create the
  flower

We call civilization. But even as we say proudly, *Look,*

Some boy at Harvard is shaping a book

Under the heavy brows of Widener and Lamont, singular and shy,

To assert the opposites of their virtue, to deny

The reek of unwanted history in the coils of their embrace,

And to search in petrol station, Hamburger Heaven, high risers,
  for the reflection of a modern face.

George Szirtes

AT THE CIRCUS 1886

No need to ask what the black horse is,
Or the dripping tinsel tickling Mamie's hair,
As she, perched delicately on her husband's knee,
Courses spirals through the blurring air.

Round and round we go, the children cry,
Next to their respectable papas;
The red-tongued horse invites their crisp applause,
The ringmaster hands round immense cigars.

We fill the sagging tent and pay no heed
To the tin clowns clattering across
The sawdust. The grey air above us bleeds –
The lollipops are cold, voluptuous.

Anthony Thwaite

OBSERVATION IN WINTER

The surfaces of earth – all rigid now
Wherever mud hardens or branches brace
Their strength against the hoar-frost as its lace
Drenches in stiffly whitened mists – show how
Things keep their postures as an accident,
Were never meant
To be seen *now* or *now*, a moment caught,
Frozen, recorded in an eyelid's shutter.
A pheasant rises, brilliant, in a flutter
Of skirling bronzes, noisily distraught,
Wrecking the field's composure.
Everything falls back startled, disarrayed,
Begins to flow again; after that brief exposure
Resumes a world that can't be stopped or stayed.

Shirley Toulson

FOR GEORGE STURT

'For I by no means perceived what a big thing I was taking so obscure a part in. In fact, more than once I tried to get clear of the business. Altogether it was so fatiguing and it bored me so.' (*The Wheelwright's Shop*, 1923)

Out of the daily boredom, he took words
And matched them to the craft
His bookish wrists could never master.
It was a skill as cunning and precise
As matching spokes to felloes, or
Hooping the red hot iron around
Dry wood, without disaster.

The Surrey farmers never knew
That they were giving orders for
Carts from a lettered man,
And one who cherished Ruskin,
Voted Labour. His pleasure was
In reasoned curves of waggon
Sides; in wheels that ran

True for their special task and land,
Right for the owner's mood and taste
In horse flesh. He delighted
In the particular, yet found
Its making heavy, cursed the waste
Of attention bent upon
Repeated detail; brought in machinery,
Sold up, and then atoned
With wheels of words, that must have cost
As much as all the days he'd gained –
                                          or lost?

Robert Vas Dias

PART OF THE STORY

There is a story I am being told by the milkman
early in the morning, crunch of gravel,
birds, the far-off sound of the surf every morning,
but this morning I am disturbed by the story
told & the milkman's ring, his apology
for disturbing me, *very sorry*, he says,
there is an incomplete story, he has
but a piece of it, *sorry*, he says, bothering
me with his apologies, I am not awake,
the story is, he can't guess my message
to him, he has but a piece of it, this is not a story,
I put a message in a bottle last night
which is not all here, there is not enough,
I know you want two pints, he says, *I can see that
from the '2', but look here*, the story begins here, I see
my message in his hand, he says, '1/2' is all
there is, is that a half of butter or half-a-dozen eggs?
– that's all there is, *that's all the snail left*, he says,
I am awake, aware of the beginning of a story
someone is trying to tell me, the thread that begins
the morning and winds through day
to penetrate night, & I try to remember
when I said I loved her,
but what had I said? – I stand there
in my pyjamas trying to remember
what I'd said to her, knowing
the message had been received, it is
as though I'd never sent it, it was long ago,
the milkman waits & I begin to be frightened
of losing my memory, my love for her,
what had I said, & how – my words swallowed
by a snail – is this possible, can such a thing
occur to me, can one say something & have it swallowed,
never to recur, was saying it to her never
to have occurred – but I say,

the snail ate through 'milk' and 'butter'
so the milkman will go away
& stop his questioning, so I can think
about the story I don't remember the beginning of,
or what has happened to
my memory which has been digested in the garden
& even now my words are spread out on a stone
slowly drying in digestive slime.

SONG OF THE FAR PLACES

Before I saw any of the postcard places
I lived among Staffordshire names and faces

before I knew which way the warm Gulf Stream went
I staged twig-races on the sickly infant Trent

I read of Mississippi bayou, fjord, calanque
and I watched the wind-stirred water from the canal bank

dreaming of wildebeeste and voortrekker
I went voyaging on a Potteries double-decker

caring nothing for sheikhdom and emirate
I cycled to Woore, Black Brook and Pipe Gate.

They told me tales of antarctic and equator
and the broad snout of the questing alligator

afloat in the jungle rivers, Orinoko and Amazon
but I watched the canal water grow dark as damson

and the turquoise dragon-flies hover and disappear:
the black tips fumed but nature was always near.

The pylons marched overhead but the long grass waved
nothing in nature was tidy or well-behaved:

I had not seen the Alps in spring blue with gentians
but I watched hedgerow lovers with their warm intentions

and though the males were hot-blooded in Brindisi
among ferns in Trentham Park they had it just as easy

and if girls were submissive in Japan and Korea
in nettle-green alleys between Longton and the Meir

they showed no more sign of prudish alarm
than their stark-naked sisters in Dar-es-Salaam.

Before I saw any of the postcard sights
I heard the loud cold wind on winter nights

throwing tiles off roofs and slashing at the trees
roaring in Penkhull as it roared in the Hebrides

and in the long summer when the baked soil hardens
the winged seeds came floating over the back gardens

teaching me what the earth is like in the burnt south
where spring water is sweeter than kisses to the mouth

for Hanley Deep Pit seemed ready to throw up lava
Trent Vale and Hanford were tropical as Java.

Yes, before I saw any of the postcard views
I knew the richness of land and water was mine to choose

which parts excited or lulled or frighteningly chilled me
or pierced my marrow with beauty or in dreams fulfilled me.

The hymnody of the earth is the same for you and for me.
Which means childhood is the same wherever you happen
to be,
except in a high-rise apartment with a colour TV.

Andrew Waterman

THE WINTER TALENT

(for Bridget O'Toole)

Fifth-Floor Pulchritude's down for a quick thrash
with the duplicator, her Antrim and my London speech
are mutually impenetrable, she doesn't drink
(inplications for God, sex?) but gave me a sweet. Looks like
pin your faith in dark knowledge of otherness, perhaps.

And Bridget has tiny stirrings for Never-mind-who,
who is spoken for; while playing the field, Des finds
Miss Riding Hood's holds only horses. The Phantom Fencer
prinks her bum through the corridors unaware
Paul spent last night on her porch in romantic stupor,

Our circus animals are all on show.
Who are these people? What will happen next?
Have we all taken leave of our senses? Is then perhaps
redeeming self-irony the stuff dreams are made on?
Just say what we all need is someone we can't talk to:

for under their duvets, or over the Bordello Rosso,
soul-mates kamikaze each other, spelling out death;
female poets are punching their lovers; ignoring the telly
('International It's a Knock-Out' in colour) they're at it
with 'I've told you before . . . ,' 'Why we married . . . ,'
    'My values . . .' All that.

While ours may be that true Shakespearian comedy world
of cross-purposes, shaping fantasies, and mistook
identities, that unfold purifyingly right.
Well then, 'Time, thou must untangle this, not I.'
So I'll buy myself a digital watch for Christmas

and live in the present. Where, through the window, bird-throngs
wheel and settle kaleidoscopically beneath neutral
sky, slaking what's left of their lusts on such worms
as the sodden ground yields, or whatever they're up to. Survival,
the winter talent. Some somehow contrive to reach summer.

Hugo Williams

TIDES

The evening advances, then withdraws again
Leaving our cups and books like islands on the floor.
We are drifting you and I,
As far from one another as the young heroes
Of these two novels we have just laid down.
For that is happiness: to wander out alone
Surrounded by the same moon, whose tides remind us of ourselves,
Our distances, and what we leave behind.
The lamp left on, the curtains letting in the light, this room.
These things were promises. No doubt we will come back to them.

A NEW WORLD SYMPHONY

What plucky sperm invented Mrs Gale?
(All starless in her first degree lay she.)

What head-of-the-river victor
plunged for her sake
down to the makings of a whale
in the amniotic sea?

Fortune the germ.
(Luck likewise it took
to get to be a sperm.)

Oh
the little bit kept its head and it flashed its tail
and there on the leaking waters –
furious, mauve, harpooned to life –
was Mrs Gale, I'm glad to say,
a beautiful daughter to Mr and Mrs Elkins,
to Mr Gale:
a bouncing wife.

Time out of mind so many minds
prized out of time to consider the light of day!
Let us rejoice in the work of the sperm
and that of the fortunate egg in Mrs. Elkins
(the role of its life to play)
who made Mrs Gale for our delight
as, happily, we
freely may.

THE CONTRIBUTORS

ANNA ADAMS was born in London. Educated mainly at art schools, she has lived in the north of England for the last twenty years. Publications of poetry include *Journey through Winter* (M.I.C.A., 1969), *A Rainbow Plantation* (Outposts, 1971), *A Memorial Tree* and *Parabola* (both from Headland, 1972 and 1975). Poems have been included in the Arts Council's *New Poems* anthologies 1 and 2 – in 1975 and 1976, and in Trevor Kneale's *Anthology of Contemporary Women Poets* and his *Poetry of the 70's* of December, 1976. Yorkshire Poets' Association 1st Prize in 1973, 1975 and 1976. Arnold Vincent Bowen Prize, from The Poetry Society, 1976.

DEBORAH ADAMS was born in 1956 and raised in Enfield, Connecticut, U.S.A. She is a student, majoring in English, at Tufts University and will graduate in 1978. She has published several poems in college anthologies and in 1976 won an Honorable Mention from the American Association of Poets.

FLEUR ADCOCK was born in Papakura, New Zealand, in 1934. She was educated at numerous schools in England and New Zealand and at Victoria University of Wellington, New Zealand, where she read Classics. Since 1963 she has been settled in London and works as a librarian in the Foreign and Common-wealth Office. Her publications include *Tigers* (1967), *High Tide in the Garden* (1971), and *The Scenic Route* (1974), all published by Oxford University Press.

KINGSLEY AMIS, born in 1922, has written three collections of poems and thirteen novels, the latest of which is *The Alteration*. He has edited *The New Oxford Book of Light Verse*, due in 1978.

JOHN ASH was born in Manchester in 1948. He went to Birmingham University where he edited a poetry magazine and was described by Richard Hoggart as 'an old-fashioned aesthete'. From there he went to Cyprus (1970) and lived there for a year, and also visited Greece, Turkey, Lebanon and Egypt. These travels had 'a decisive influence'. Apart from tirelessly pursuing antiquities (nine Greco-Roman cities on the south coast of Turkey alone) he met for the first time Odious Rich People. He returned to Manchester in 1971 where he has lived ever since. He began collaboration with Louis Turner (of the Royal Institute of International Affairs) on various projects critical of capitalism, culminating in *The Golden Hordes* (pub. Constable 1975) – a criticism of international tourism. At present unemployed, living in Disdbury (for the sake or its Orchid House) and working on *The Mauve Book: In Praise of Decadence*. He reads very little English poetry at all. Favourite living poet – Yannis Ritsos. Favourite poet – Laforgue.

GEORGE BARKER was born in 1913, self- and travel-educated and lives in Norfolk. He has taught in Japan and America and written fiction and children's verse. His first book of poems was published by David Archer in 1934. His most recent collection, *Dialogues, etc.* was a Poetry Book Society Choice in 1976.

ELIZABETH BARTLETT is married, with two step-children and one child of her own. Educated at what was then known as an elementary school, and then at a grammar school in Dover – on one of the first batch of scholarships offered to working-class children – she left at the age of fifteen and worked in a hypodermic needle factory, a garage, a bank, and is now a medical secretary and on the committee of the local W.E.A. She has had poems published in many literary magazines during the last twenty-five years.

PATRICIA BEER was born in Devon in 1924 and educated at Exmouth Grammar School, Exeter University and St Hugh's College, Oxford. She taught in universities in Italy and England for some years and is now a full-time writer. She has published four books of poems, the most recent being *The Estuary* (Macmillan, 1971) and *Driving West* (Gollancz, 1975). Her most recent critical book is *Reader, I Married Him* (Macmillan, 1974). She has also written an autobiography of childhood, *Mrs Beer's House* (Macmillan, 1968), and was the editor of *New Poems, 1975*. She reviews for the *T.L.S.*, *The Listener* and *The New York Times*. She is married to an architect and lives in Hampstead and Devon.

CONNIE BENSLEY was born and (grammar school educated) in south-west London. She has two adolescent sons. She has worked for an M.P., doctors, an author – mostly as a secretary. She writes chiefly about people, and about the poor jokes of which they tend to be victims.

JAMES BERRY was born in Jamaica. He lived four years in America before coming to London. He has given many broadcast talks and seminars on growing up in the West Indies and on race relations. He reads his short stories on radio and has had a radio play produced. He has contributed regularly to the Barbadian literary magazine BIM, and the journal of the Caribbean Artists Movement SAVACOU. His poems have also appeared in *The Listener*, *London Magazine*, *Poetry Review*, *Tribune*, *Limestone Magazine*, *New Poetry*, other magazines and anthologies. He has published short stories and articles. He organizes readings and reads with the Bluefoot Travellers, and he read at the Caribbean Festival of the Arts, Jamaica, in 1976. He organized the Jamaica 10th and 12th Independence Anniversary Festival readings and the poetry section *Notting Hill Carnival Exhibition* at the I.C.A. He has published a small selection of his poetry, *Lucy's Letter*, 1975, and edited an anthology of U.K. West Indian poetry, *Bluefoot Traveller*, published in 1976.

THOMAS BLACKBURN was born in Cumberland in 1916 and recently retired from his position as lecturer in English at a London college. His eighth and most recent book of poems was *Selected Poems*, Hutchinson. He also recently published a collection of poems for fifth and sixth forms, *The Devil's Kitchen* (Chatto & Windus). His hobby was mountaineering but later mountain walking, and he was proud of having introduced Christian Bonington to the sport. He died in August 1977.

PETER BLAND was born in 1934 in Scarborough. He emigrated to New Zealand in 1954 and became well known there as poet, actor, and co-founder of Wellington's first professional theatre. He returned to London in 1969 with his family and works as a freelance writer/actor. His first English collection of poetry *Mr Maui* (London Magazine Editions) was a recent Poetry Book Society Recommendation.

IAN BOWMAN was born in 1915 in Princeton, New Jersey. He was educated at Princeton schools, Glasgow High School, Glasgow University and Queen's College, Oxford (Indian Studies). From 1937 to 1947 he was in the Indian Civil Service (1942–3 seconded to Indian Army, active service Assam–Burma border and Arakan, in ' V' Force. Rank of Captain). From 1947 to 1948 he worked as a coal miner at Balmore Colliery under an N.C.B. recruitment scheme. He has held posts as Assistant Registrar, University of Liverpool; Registrar at University College, Ibadan, Nigeria; lecturer in Classics at University College, Ibadan, and at Nigerian College of Arts, Science and Technology, Ibadan (1948–54). He taught Classics at Hyndland Secondary School, Glasgow (1955–61), and was a lecturer in Liberal Studies at Mining Institute, Falkirk. Now Head of Department of General Studies at Falkirk College of Technology, he is married, with two daughters, and is also a J.P. He is interested in Industrial History, Archaeology, Music (organist and piper). His book of poetry *Orientations*, was published by Akros Publications in 1977.

EDWIN BROCK was born in London in 1927 and now lives in Norfolk. Since his first collection in 1959 he has published seven further volumes in this country and in America, the most recent being *Song of the battery hen* (Selected Poems 1959–75) and *Here. Now. Always.*, an autobiographical sequence of prose and poetry, both published by Secker & Warburg. He has been Poetry Editor of *Ambit* for thirteen years, and a selection of his poetry appears in the Penguin Modern Poets series (No. 8).

BALFOUR BROWN was born in Greenock and now lives in Ayrshire. He teaches English and writes poems and short stories.

ALAN BROWNJOHN was born in 1931 and educated at London elementary and grammar schools and Merton College, Oxford. Among his volumes of poetry are *The Railings* (1961), *The Lions' Mouths* (1967), *Brownjohn's Beasts* (1970) and *A Song of Good Life* (1975).

CAROL BRUGGEN was born in Blackburn, Lancashire, in 1932. She was educated at Wycombe Abbey, University College of the South-West, Exeter, and St Katharine's College, Liverpool. She has been married for twenty years with a son and daughter, living in a Lancashire village, writing, sometimes teaching, and bringing up her family. Her poems have been published by the Mid-Pennine Association, Quill Books and little magazines.

JIM BURNS was born in Preston. His major collections are *A Single Flower* (Andium Press, 1972); *Leben in Preston* (Palmenpresse, Germany, 1973); *The Goldfish Speaks From Beyond The Grave* (Salamander Imprint, 1976). A frequent contributor to *Tribune*, he has also had poems, stories and reviews published in *Ambit*, *Poetry Information*, *The Industrial Unionist*, *Samphire*, and many others.

JACK CAREY, born in Bristol, is married with two children and lectures at the Polytechnic of North London. His poems have been published in a few magazines and a collection *Woods and Mirrors* by Salamander Imprint, 1976. A long poem, *The Cathedral*, was published as a booklet by Workshop New Poetry in 1973.

CHARLES CAUSLEY was born at Launceston, Cornwall, and, apart from the war years, has spent most of his life there. He taught in his native town for many years and was Visiting Fellow in Poetry at the University of Exeter 1973–4. A Fellow of the Royal Society of Literature, he was awarded the Queen's Gold Medal for Poetry in 1967. In 1976 he resigned his teaching post and is now a full-time writer. In 1977, Exeter University conferred on him the Honourary Degree of Doctor of Letters. His books include *Collected Poems* (Macmillan, 1975), *The Hill of the Fairy Calf* (Hodder & Stoughton, 1976), and Macmillan will publish *The Animals' Carol* in 1978. In 1975, Sentinel Records produced the LP: 'Causley Reads Causley' (Sens 1028).

CAL CLOTHIER was born in Portsmouth in 1940 and read English at New College, Oxford. He won the Guinness International Poetry Prize in 1971 and has published in most leading

British magazines and in many leading anthologies. His books include *Love Time* (1973), *Behind Heslington Hall* (1973) and *Headhunters* (1974), and a selection of his work will appear in *Poetry Introduction 4* (Faber & Faber, 1978). He is a principal lecturer in Humanities and Contemporary Studies at Leeds Polytechnic.

STEWART CONN is married with two small sons and lives in Edinburgh. *An Ear to the Ground* was the choice of the Poetry Book Society. A new volume *Under the Ice* is due from Hutchinson next year. He edited *New Poems 1973–4*. His plays include *The King, The Burning Thistlewood*, and *Play Donkey*.

ROSALIND CONWAY was born in London in 1954. She has also lived in various places in the U.S. and in Ottawa, where she did a B.A. and an M.A. in English at Carleton University.

ELSIE CRANMER was born in 1893 in North London, daughter of an architect and surveyor, A.R.I.B.A., receiving the usual middle-class education. She had been intended for a musical career but, owing to eye trouble at the time she should have been studying for a degree, gave up the idea. After an interval, during which she married, she turned to writing short stories (never published). After her husband was killed in World War I she got on to the staff of *The Poetry Review* by writing a piece of poetic prose, but she was not able to write poetry until she dreamed, in the early morning (in a semi-conscious state) a whole poem which she sent to a periodical edited by G. K. Chesterton. It was published with other later poems, and she contributed to most of the literary periodicals of that time. She is a Baha'i by conviction and has spent many years working, writing and teaching for this faith.

ADELE DAVID was born in Manchester and educated in England, America and Canada. She studied painting and has taught in art colleges, but she now teaches art therapy and literature. She lives in London with her two daughters. Her poems have appeared in various magazines.

DOUGLAS DUNN was born in 1942, at Inchinnan, Scotland. His books are: *Terry Street* (1969), *The Happier Life* (1972), and *Love or Nothing* (1974). He wrote a radio play *Scotsmen by Moonlight* (1977). Recent verse includes a commentary for *Early Every Morning* (B.B.C. Schools TV) and a series of poems for an Omnibus film about runners and athletics.

D. J. ENRIGHT taught for over twenty years in the East and now works in publishing. His publications include *Memoirs of a Mendicant Professor* (1969), *Selected Poems* (1969), *Man is an Onion*, literary essays (1972), and the following volumes of poetry, *Daughters of Earth* (1972), *The Terrible Shears* (1973) and *Sad Ires* (1975).

U. A. FANTHORPE was born in Kent in 1929 and educated in Surrey and at Oxford. She taught for sixteen years, but found it impossible to combine this with writing so she abandoned responsibility and its Burnham scale in favour of a 9–5 job and freedom to think. She now works as a clerk in a Bristol hospital.

ELAINE FEINSTEIN was born in 1930. Her publications include three books of poems, *In a green eye*, *The Magic Apple Tree*, and *The Celebrants*, and a new book of selected poems, *Some Unease and Angels*, appeared in 1977. She has translated the poems of Tsvetayeva for O.U.P. and Penguin. Four of her novels, *The Circle*, *The Amberstone Exit*, *The Crystal Garden* and *Children of the Rose* are available in Penguin. Her latest novel is *The Ecstasy of Dr Miriam Garner*. She is married, with three sons, and lives in Cambridge.

JAMES FENTON published one book of poems, *Terminal Moraine*, ages ago. He is now writing a book about Cambodia and Vietnam for the same publisher (Secker & Warburg). He was born in 1949 and is living in London.

MICHAEL FOLEY was born in 1947 in Derry and educated there and at Queen's University, Belfast, where he did research and edited *The Honest Ulsterman*, leaving in 1972 to work as a teacher in London. He has one collection of poems, *True Life Love Stories* (Blackstaff Press, 1976), and a collection of short stories is due in late 1977.

RICHARD FREEMAN is thirty-nine years old. He was born in Chester, but grew up in Laleham-on-Thames, spending most of his childhood in, on or by the river. He was educated at Ashford County Grammar School and Mill Hill School. He spent two years in Germany to learn the language and has travelled widely in the Far East. He is now a freelance writer, scripting and producing commercial and documentary films, copywriting, etc. He has published one book of poems, *The Rain That Eats* (Arts Printing, Malaysia), while living in Kuala Lumpur. He admits to being obsessively interested in megalithic culture. He resides in Putney with a wife and daughter.

JOHN FULLER has published six collections of poems, the latest being *The Mountain in the Sea* (Secker and Warburg, 1975). He has also published a number of works for children, and some criticism. He is married, with three daughters, and lives in Oxford.

ROY FULLER was born in 1912. His latest book is *Poor Roy*, poems for children and others. With the late Clifford Dyment and Montagu Slater he edited the first P.E.N. anthology in 1952.

ROBIN FULTON was born in Scotland in 1937 and now lives in Scandinavia. Collections of his poetry include *The Spaces between the Stones* (New Rivers Press, New York, 1971), *The Man with the Surbahar* (Macdonald, Edinburgh, 1971), *Tree-Lines* (New Rivers Press, New York, 1974) and *Between Flights* (Interim Press, Surrey, 1977). Swedish poets he has translated include Lars Gustafsson (New Rivers Press, New York, 1972), Gunnar Harding (London Magazine Editions, London 1973), Tomas Tranströmer (Penguin Books, London, 1974), Östen Sjöstrand (Oleander Press, Cambridge and New York, 1975) and Werner Aspenström (Oasis Books, London, 1976). He has also published *Contemporary Scottish Poetry: Individuals and Contexts* (Macdonald, Edinburgh, 1974). He edited thirty-seven issues of the quarterly *Lines Review* (Macdonald, Edinburgh) between 1967 and 1976, and the associated Lines Review Editions. He held the Writer's Fellowship at Edinburgh University from 1969 to 1971.

LEWIS GARDNER is an American poet and playwright who was born in 1943. He has worked as a teacher and editor, and he was educated at Columbia University and University of Chicago. His poem 'At The Maytag' is a true story. His play *Hot Dimes* will appear in New York in 1977.

GEOFFREY GRIGSON lives in Swindon and since 1939 has published many collections of poetry including *Under the Cliff and other poems* (1943), *Places of the Mind* (1949), *Collected Poems* (1963) and *Discoveries of Bones and Stones and Other Poems* (1971) which received the Duff Cooper Memorial Prize in 1972. He edited the *Faber Book of Popular Verse* (1971) and the *Faber Book of Love Poems* (1973). His most recent books are *The Contrary View* (1974) and *Britain Observed* (1975).

MADGE HALES was born and brought up in the country, where she attended a small school when able as illness prevented much learning. She later took book-keeping and extra-mural work in Nottingham for some years, studying English and American literature, poetry, psychology, under Mr Wiltshire, who was instrumental in starting the Open University on the B.B.C. She has published two collections of poetry (Chatto & Windus) and a pamphlet from Nottingham University, and appears regularly in periodicals and on Radio 3, Poetry Now, New Poetry, etc. Also short stories (on Third), light satire. She edited jointly *The Glass*, which published the first efforts of Bernard Kops, Harold Pinter, Tom Blackburn, etc. She is married and has one son and one daughter.

TONY HARRISON was born in Leeds in 1937. He spent four years in Northern Nigeria and a year in Prague before returning to England to become the first Northern Arts Fellow in Poetry, 1967–8, a position he held a second time in 1976–7. In 1969 he received the Cholmondeley Award for Poetry and the UNESCO Fellowship in Poetry which took him to Cuba, Brazil, Senegal and the Gambia. His collection of poems *The Loiners* (London Magazine Editions, 1970) was awarded the Geoffrey Faber Memorial Prize 1972. His most recent publications include the two texts for the National Theatre, *The Misanthrope* (Rex Collings, 1973), *Phaedra Britannica* (Rex Collings, 1975); *Palladas: Poems*

(Anvil Press/Rex Collings, 1975) and *Ten Poems from The School of Eloquence* (Rex Collings Christmas Book, 1976). He has also done English lyrics for music by Mikis Theodorakis, lyrics for U.S./U.S.S.R. co-production of *The Blue Bird*, working in Leningrad with George Cukor; a new English libretto for Smetana's *Prodaná Nevêsta* for the Metropolitan Opera, New York. He is currently working on the *Oresteia* of Aeschylus for the new Olivier Theatre of the National Theatre for 1978.

IAN HARROW lives in North Yorkshire and lectures on Art History. His poems have been published in *London Magazine*, *Stand*, *English* and *Twenty Years of Poetry and Audience*. 'Novel as Biography' is one of a sequence of thirty poems entitled 'Colonus'.

FRANCIS HARVEY was born in Enniskillen, Northern Ireland, but has lived most of his life in Donegal in the Republic – a county whose landscape and people have been a major inspiration to him. His work has appeared in leading Irish literary periodicals, but he has not published a collection. He is also a playwright whose radio plays have been broadcast by R.T.E., B.B.C., and European radio stations. He is a lover of remote places – mountain summits and western islands. He is married with five daughters.

S. L. HENDERSON SMITH was born in 1919 in North China. Formerly a medical missionary in China and Africa, he is now a general practitioner at Huddersfield. He has published six books of poetry, the most recent being *Filterings*, Outposts Publications (1975). He is an enthusiast for Voluntary Euthanasia, Conservation, Recycling, Bee-Keeping. He is a sub-editor of *Envoi* and president of the Pennine Poets. He sees poetry as modern man's substitute for religion.

PHOEBE HESKETH was born in Preston, Lancashire, and educated in Southport and at Cheltenham Ladies' College. She was elected an F.R.S.L. in 1971. She was the Woman's Page Editor of *Bolton Evening News* (1942–5) and a freelance journalist. She is also a script-writer for the B.B.C. and a lecturer in schools and colleges. She is on the Arts Council Panel: Poets Reading

Poems. Twice winner of Greenwood Prize for Poetry, she has published eight volumes of verse. She has also written a biography: *My Aunt Edith* (1966) and *Rivington* (a Country Book Club Choice, 1974).

DAVID HOLBROOK was born in 1923 in Norwich. He is author of a number of well-known books on education, and has published a novel, four volumes of verse, and studies in the psychology of culture. *Lost Bearings in English Poetry* appeared in 1977 and scheduled for later publication are *A Play of Passion*, a novel, and *Education, Nihilism and Survival*. He is married with four children and lives near Cambridge.

LIBBY HOUSTON was born in North London in 1941 of Scottish ancestry and brought up in Somerset. She read English at Oxford and has been writing and giving public readings for many years. She appeared at the Rotterdam Poetry International 1973 and was awarded an Arts Council grant in 1972. She has worked variously in publishing and has written poetry programmes for B.B.C. Schools. She lives in London with her two children. Her published collections are: *A Stained Glass Raree Show* and *Plain Clothes*, both Allison & Busby.

TED HUGHES was born in Mytholmroyd, West Yorkshire, in 1930, and from Mexborough Grammar School went to Pembroke College, Cambridge. His publications include: *The Hawk in the Rain* (1957), *Lupercal* (1960), *Meet My Folks!* (1961), *The Earth-Owl and Other Moon People* (1963), *How the Whale Became* (1963), *Nessie the Mannerless Monster* (1964), *Wodwo* (1967), *Poetry in the Making* (1968), *The Iron Man* and *Crow* (1970); his most recent books are *Season Songs* and *Gaudete*.

BRIAN JONES. Volumes of his published poetry include *Poems, A Family Album, Interior* and *For Mad Mary*, all published by Alan Ross L.M.E. Editions. Also, *The Spitfire on the Northern Line*, in Chatto's *Poetry for the Young* series. He has received an Eric Gregory Award, and a Cholmondeley Award for poetry. His work has been featured in anthologies such as the Penguin *English Poetry since 1945, Breakthrough, The Living Poet* and *The Younger British Poets*. He was educated at Cambridge and now lives in Canterbury.

JENNY KING was born in London in 1940, studied English at Cambridge and now lives in Sheffield. She is married to a medieval historian and has two children. She has had poems in *Outposts, The Tablet, Stand, English, Encounter, Workshop, Blackwood's Magazine* and *The Critical Quarterly*.

LINCOLN KIRSTEIN was born in 1907 in Rochester, New York, and educated at Philips Exeter Academy and Harvard University. He is now the director of the New York City Ballet. His published work includes, *Dance, a Short History*; *Movement & Metaphor*; *Nijinsky* and *Rhymes of a Pfc*.

DAVID LAN was born in 1952. He is an established playwright and plays of his that have been performed are *Painting a Wall* (1974), *Bird Child* (1974), *Paradise* (1975), *Homage to Been Soup* (1975), *The Winter Dancers* (1977), all but the first at the Royal Court Theatre. He has had poems published in *Ambit*.

JAMES LAUGHLIN was born in 1914, and has been the editor of New Directions Books in New York since 1936. His *Selected Poems* are in print with Gaberbocchus Press in London.

B. C. LEALE was born in Ashford, Middlesex, in 1930 and educated at the Municipal College, Southend. He is employed as a bookseller's assistant and lives in London. Two booklets of his early poems *Under a Glass Sky* (1975) and *Preludes* (1977) have been published by Caligula Books.

LAURENCE LERNER was born in Cape Town in 1925, and educated at the University of Cape Town and Pembroke College, Cambridge. He has taught English at the University of Ghana and Queen's University, Belfast, and more briefly in Dijon, various American universities and Munich, where he first saw Guardi's painting of a Venetian Gala Concert; he is now at the University of Sussex. His publications include *The Englishmen* (a novel), *The Truest Poetry* (a critical work), and four books of poetry, *Domestic Interior* (1959), *The Directions of Memory* (1964), *Selves* (1969) and *A.R.T.H.U.R.* (1974). Further publications consist of a second novel, *A Free Man* (1968), and three further books of criticism, *The Truthtellers* (1967), *The Uses of Nostalgia* (1972) and *Introduction to English Poetry* (1975).

PAMELA LEWIS was born in Nottingham, trained as an Occupational Therapist in London and is now married with three children, living in her home town. Her first collection *One Mile From The Centre* was published by Turret Books, 1971. Her poems have been broadcast on B.B.C. Radio 3 and 4 and on Northern Drift, and have been included in the anthologies *Shapes and Creatures* by Geoffrey Grigson and *Impetus* (Ginn & Co.). She has been published in *Cornhill, Encounter, English, The Magazine, I.C.A., Omens, Poetry Review, Samphire, Workshop* and *The Listener*.

DINAH LIVINGSTONE was born Tokyo 1940 and brought up in the English countryside. She studied in Paris and Innsbruck (theology). She came to Camden Town in 1966 and lives there with three children. She has given many poetry readings, broadcast and live, published in magazines and anthologies and earns a living by adult education poetry classes and translating (French, German, Spanish, Italian). She has received two Arts Council Awards (1969 and 1970) for her poems: *beginning* (1967), *tohu bohu* (1968), *maranatha* (1969), Lorca and John of the Cross translations (1969), *Holy city of London* (1970), *captivity captive* (1971) and *Ultrasound*, (1974) published by Katabasis, 10 St Martins Close, London NW1.

LIZ LOCHHEAD was born in Motherwell, Lanarkshire, in 1947, and was trained in the drawing and printing department of Glasgow School of Art, where she became perversely committed to poetry. Her first collection, *Memo for Spring* (Reprographia, Edinburgh, 1972), won the Arts Council New Writing Award. Her work has appeared in several anthologies (*Scottish Poetry Six, Seven, Eight, Nine. Made In Scotland*, Carcanet, 1974) and magazines. She lives in Glasgow and works as teacher of Art in a large comprehensive school.

MICHAEL LONGLEY was born in Belfast in 1939 and was educated in Belfast and Dublin. He is now Assistant Director of the Arts Council of Northern Ireland. Collections of poetry are *No Continuing City* (1969), *An Exploded View* (1973) and *Man Lying on a Wall* (1976), and he has a selection in *Penguin Modern Poets 26.*

GEORGE MACBETH is now a novelist as well as a poet His latest work of fiction, *The Survivor*, came out last summer.

ROY McFADDEN was born in Belfast in 1921. He is a poet. and a lawyer, and his published work is: *Swords and Ploughshares* (1943), *Flowers for a Lady* (1945), *The Heart's Townland* (1947), *Elegy for the Dead of the Princess Victoria* (1952), *The Garryowen* (1971) and *Verifications* (1977). *Impostors* is one of a sequence of poems dealing with judicial violence.

JEAN MACVEAN lives in London, is divorced and has two children. She has published some poems under the title *Ideas of Love* and a novel *The Intermediaries*, a modern version of the Tristan and Isolde legend. Her poems have appeared in *Encounter*, *Poetry of the Seventies* (Rondo Publications), the Mandeville Press, and the *Tablet*.

WES MAGEE was born in 1939 in Greenock, Scotland. His publications include *Poetry Introduction 2* (Faber, 1972) and *Urban Gorilla* (Leeds University Press, 1973). His poems have appeared in four previous P.E.N. anthologies. He received a Literature Bursary award from Southern Arts Association in 1977.

FARIDA MAJID. Born in a literary family in pre-independence Calcutta, Farida Majid wrote poetry in Bengali from an early age and was published widely in Bengali magazines until her marriage to an American architect. Between travelling with her internationally active husband she managed to read English at New York University, graduated with honours in 1971. Since her divorce in 1973 she has been living in England and began to write in English. She set up the Salamander Imprint in 1973 which has since then published several highly acclaimed books of poetry. Her own publications include *From Inside the Prison Camp*, and *Take Me Home, Rickshaw*, both collections of poems translated from contemporary poetry of Bangladesh.

DERWENT MAY, who was born in 1930, is the literary editor of *The Listener*. He was the co-editor, with James Price, of *Oxford Poetry 1952*, and is the author of three novels, *The Professionals* (1964), *Dear Parson* (1969) and *The Laughter in Djakarta* (1973). He is married, with a son and a daughter, and lives in Regent's Park.

GERDA MAYER was born in 1927 in Carlsbad, Czechoslovakia. She came to England in 1939 and was educated at Bedford College, London. Selections of her poems were published in *Gerda Mayer's Library Folder* (All-In, 1972), and *Treble Poets 2* (Chatto & Windus, 1975). *The Knockabout Show* will be published in 1978 in the Chatto Poets for the Young Series.

ROGER MITCHELL was born in Boston, Massachusetts. He did graduate work at Manchester University in the early sixties. His two books of poetry are *Letters From Siberia and Other Poems* (1971) and *Moving* (1976). He now teaches at Indiana University, edits *The Minnesota Review*, and helps raise his two daughters.

JOHN MOLE was born in 1941, brought up in Somerset, and now lives in Hertfordshire where he writes, teaches and is an editor (with Peter Scupham) for the Mandeville Press, Hitchin. He reviews for *The Listener* and *Times Literary Supplement*, and his most recent collection of poems is *Our Ship* (Secker & Warburg). He is married with two sons.

ABIGAIL MOZLEY was born in 1947 and educated in Berkshire, Kuala Lumpur and Penzance. She has been published in *Little Word Machine*, *Ambit*, *Xenia*, *Gallery* and *Poetry Workshop*, among others, and is a contributor to *Women Poets' Anthology 1975* and Poetry Now (B.B.C. 3), 1974. She read at London Poetry Society, 1976. She is married with two children and lives in Falmouth and Cambridge (mature undergraduate reading Eng. Lit.). Her other activities are usheretting and journalism.

ANGUS NICOLSON was born in the Isle of Skye, which he left when sixteen. He spent $7\frac{1}{2}$ (eternal) years as railway clerk.

He was educated at Glasgow University (1968–71) and edited student magazine *Gum*. He has published regularly in Gaelic quarterly *Gairm* and in various Scottish, Irish and American magazines. The usual variety of jobs includes, latterly, $3\frac{1}{2}$ years as a housing officer in London. He is now Gaelic Writer in Residence based at Sabhal Mor Ostaig, South Skye. He is currently member of General Council of the Poetry Society and National Poetry Centre.

JEFF NUTTALL was born in 1933 and trained at art school as a painter and now teaches full-time in the Fine Art Department, Leeds Poly. He has had his painting and sculpture exhibited by the Angela Flowers Gallery. He is also deeply involved in Performance Art as a writer of scenarios and, until recently, as a performer with Rose McGuire. Verse, fiction and something in between the two, involving drawings and collage, was published by Unicorn Writers Forum, Aloes Press, *Penguin Modern Poets No. 12* (with Jackson and Wantling), Fulcrum, Trigram and Poet and Peasant. He recently enjoyed a brief but stormy period as Chairman of the Council of the National Poetry Society until he resigned in disgust, with great relief. He is currently engaged on a biography of verteran comedian Frank Randle.

SEAN O'HUIGIN was born in Brampton, Ontario, in 1942. He is the co-founder of the New Writers' Workshop, Toronto. He has been involved in film and stage production, recording of electronic music and poetry and experimental poetry workshops for schools. He was the poet in residence at Vauxhall Manor Secondary School (1974–6). He has read and worked with Bob Cobbing in International Festivals of Sound Poetry and organized National Festival of Poetry For and By Children (London, 1976). Collections of his poetry are *sean o'huigin* (Pirate Press, 1974), *Henry Morgan's Delicate Balance* (Good Elf, 1975), *Octodecimo/huigin* (M.H.I.C., Toronto, 1970).

FRANK ORMSBY was born in 1947 in County Fermanagh. He graduated from Queen's University, Belfast, in 1971 and now lives in Belfast with his wife and two children. He is Head Master of the English Department at Royal Belfast Academical Institution and edits *The Honest Ulsterman*. He won a Gregory Award in 1974. A selection of his poems appeared in *Ten Irish Poets*, Carcanet Press, and his first full-length collection, *A Store of Candles*, O.U.P., is out this autumn.

ROSIE ORR was born in 1946 and studied graphic design at Hornsey College of Art. She is now living and working in Oxford.

TREVOR PALLISTER is thirty-nine, still married and predictable. For a few years to 1974 his poetry was acceptable to *Phoenix*, *Second Aeon*, *The Honest Ulsterman* and others. For his living he teaches science to children of all colours, creeds and smells.

BRIAN LOUIS PEARCE was born in Acton in 1933. He was a deacon at the Acton Baptist Church, 1961–8, and the chairman of the Twickenham Christian Council, 1974–5. He is the librarian of Richmond upon Thames College and sometime Senior Examiner for the Library Association in Literature in English. He is also Chairman of the Richmond Poetry Group and Editor of the *Quarto Poetry Series*. His publications include poetry, criticism, plays, and educational, local, and family history. His *Selected Poems, 1951–1973*, is due shortly. He has been a contributor to many journals and anthologies including *Expression Poetry Quarterly*, *Green River Review*, *The Guardian*, *Littack*, *New Poems 1976–77*, *Outposts*, *Poesie Vivante*, *Poetry Review* and *Tribune*.

PETER PORTER is an Australian, resident in London since 1951. He has published six volumes of poems, including *Living in a Calm Country* (O.U.P., 1975), *Versions of Martial's Epigrams* and several other books. He is a freelance writer, reviewer and broadcaster.

W. PRICE TURNER was born in 1927 at York. His published collections are: *First Offence*, *The Rudiment of an Eye*, *The Flying Corset*, *Fables from Life*, *More Fables from Life* and *The Moral Rocking-Horse*. He has had six novels (as Bill Turner) published here and abroad. He was Gregory Fellow in Poetry at Leeds University 1960–2, and Creative Fellow at Glasgow University 1973–5. He now teaches creative writing.

CRAIG RAINE was born in 1944 and educated at Exeter College, Oxford. A freelance academic and journalist, he is currently lecturer in English at Christ Church, Oxford, and writes for the *New Statesman*, *The New Review* and the *London Magazine*, among others. A selection of his poems will appear in Faber's *Poetry Introduction 4* (Jan. 1978) and his first collection, *The Onion, Memory*, will be published by Oxford University Press in May 1978.

PETER READING was born in 1946 and trained as a painter at Liverpool College of Art. His collections *For the Municipality's Elderly* (1974), *The Prison Cell & Barrel Mystery* (Poetry Book Society recommendation for spring 1976) and *Nothing for Anyone* (1977) are published by Secker & Warburg.

PETER REDGROVE's books of verse include *From Every Chink of the Ark* (Routledge 1977). He has also published several novels, has had plays performed on the radio, and has written with Penelope Shuttle a feminist book on menstruation: *The Wise Wound: Eve's Curse and Everywoman* due out from Gollancz next year. He read Science at Cambridge and has worked as Visiting Poet to Buffalo University, as Gregory Fellow at Leeds University, and Professor of Literature at Colgate University. He is at present Resident Author at the Falmouth School of Art, and lives and works in collaboration with Penelope Shuttle. Their daughter Theresa was born in 1976.

HARRIET ROSE is working on a show based on her book, *The Steel Circle* (Gallery Publications), a tarot sequence illustrated by David Hayhow. She has completed several sequences of poems and three novels and is widely published in magazines and anthologies including *Arts Council Anthology*, *Confrontation*, *Cosmopolitan*, *Tree*, *Contemporary Women Poets*, *Poems of the 70s*, *Akros*, *Pinks Peace*, *Meridian*, *Gallery* and *New Poetry*. She is part of a women's poetry theatre troup called The Prodigal Daughters performing at Pentameters, The Little Theatre, Cockpit Theatre, University of Sussex and Action Space, among others. She is also interested in the danced poem and studies dance.

CAROL RUMENS was born in Forest Hill, has always lived in and around South London. She was educated at grammar school and read Philosophy for a short time at London University. She has one collection of poems so far, *A Strange Girl in Bright Colours* (Quartet, 1973). Her work has been broadcast by B.B.C. 2 and published in such periodicals as *Stand, Encounter, The Listener, The Honest Ulsterman, Bananas, T.L.S.* and *The Sunday Times.*

VERNON SCANNELL was born in 1922 and is a freelance writer. His most recent publications are: *The Tiger and the Rose,* an autobiography (Hamish Hamilton); *Selected Poems* (Allison & Busby); *The Winter Man,* poems (Allison & Busby); and *The Apple Raid,* poems for children (Chatto & Windus). *The Loving Game* (Robson Books) was a Poetry Book Society Choice for 1975 and *Not Without Glory* (Woburn Press), a critical book on British and American poetry of the Second World War, was published in 1976. *A Proper Gentleman,* 1977, a prose account of the life of a Writer in Residence (Robson Books), is his latest work.

SUSAN SCHAEFFER is thirty-six and a Full Professor at Brooklyn College. She received her B.A., M.A. and Ph.D. from the University of Chicago. She has published two novels, *Falling* and *Anya* (Macmillan, U.S., Cassells, England). *Anya* won both the Friends of Literature Award and the Edward Lewis Wallant Award. She has published four volumes of poetry: *The Witch and the Weather Report* (1972), *Granite Lady* (1975), a National Book Award Nominee, *Rhymes and Runes of the Toad* (1976, all published by Macmillan), and *Alphabet for the Lost Years* (Gallimaufry, 1977). She has had poetry published in *Cosmopolitan, Esquire, Ms., Mademoiselle* and most small magazines in England and America. Doubleday will be publishing her next novel, *Time in Its Flight,* and her next book of poems, *Bible of the Beasts of the Little Field,* in 1977.

PENELOPE SHUTTLE was born near London in 1947. She has published novels and collections of poetry, the most recent being *Rainsplitter in the Zodiac Garden,* a novel (Calder & Boyars), and *Webs of Fire,* poetry (Gallery Press). Forthcoming books include *The Mirror of the Giant,* a novel, and *The Candlemas*

Notebook, poems. Work in progress includes a novel, *In the Winter*; and, with Peter Redgrove, a non-fiction book on the psychology of menstruation, *The Wise Wound: Eve's Curse and Everywoman*. She now lives and works in collaboration with Peter Redgrove in Cornwall.

JAMES SIMMONS was born in Derry in 1933 and went to Leeds University. He has published six collections of verse, the most recent *July Garland and The Cold War* (Blackstaff Press, Belfast, 1976). His *Selected Poems* is being brought out this year simultaneously in Ireland and America. He founded *The Honest Ulsterman* in 1968 and The Poor Genius Record Company in 1976. A film devoted to his life and work was shown on Omnibus in January 1976. He teaches at the New University of Ulster, Coleraine, and gives many concerts of his songs and poems. He has written three plays.

C. H. SISSON was born in Bristol, 1914, and educated at the University of Bristol and in France and Germany. He wasted many years in the Civil Service and a few in the army. He now lives in Somerset, and has written novels, critical works, translations and a book on public administration. His publications inclued *In the Trojan Ditch*, collected poems and selected translations (Carcanet Press, 1974), and *Anchises*, new poems (1976).

KNUTE SKINNER was born in St Louis, Missouri, and studied at Culver-Stockton College, Colorado State, Middlebury College, and the University of Iowa. Skinner wandered around Europe before dividing his residence between Ireland and America. In Ireland he lives in a cottage in rural County Clare. In America he teaches at Western Washington State College, where he is presently a professor of English. His books include *Stranger with a Watch*, *A Close Sky over Killaspuglonane*, and *The Sorcerers*. He is an editor of *The Bellingham Review*. His honours include a creative writing fellowship from the National Endowment for the Arts.

JULIAN SYMONS was born in London in 1912. He made a reputation before the Second World War as editor of *Twentieth Century Verse*, a magazine which published most of the young poets outside the immediate Auden circle. Today he is known as a crime novelist, biographer, and social and military historian. He has written over thirty books, including two collections of verse, writes TV plays and regularly reviews for *The Sunday Times*. He enjoys watching football and cricket and wandering about cities.

GEORGE SZIRTES was born in Budapest in 1948 and emigrated to England in 1956. He trained as an artist in Leeds and London. His poems have been widely published in anthologies and magazines including *The Listener, Encounter, T.L.S.* and *New Statesman* since 1972 but chiefly in the last year. He has two pamphlet collections, *Poems* (Perkins, 1972), *The Iron Clouds* (Dodman, 1975), and a limited edition of etchings and poems *Visitors* (Mandeville, 1976). A selection of poems is due to appear in Faber's *Poetry Introduction 4*. Forthcoming is a further set of etchings and poems, *An Illustrated Alphabet* (Mandeville). He has also written and produced two verse plays for children: *The Bee Boy of Selbourne* and *Cauchemar*.

ANTHONY THWAITE was born in 1930. He has taught in universities in Japan and Libya, worked as a B.B.C. producer, was literary editor of *The Listener* and later of the *New Statesman*, and is now co-editor of *Encounter*. He has published six books of poems, most recently *A Portion for Foxes*, Oxford University Press, 1977, and a selection in the Penguin Modern Poets series.

SHIRLEY TOULSON was born in 1924 and educated at Birkbeck College, London. She works as a freelance journalist and writer, and until 1974 specialized almost entirely in education topics. Since that date she has also written on aspects of rural social history. She is currently engaged in research for a book on the relevance of poetry to today's 'common reader', for which she has received an Arts Council grant. Her poems and short stories have appeared in various literary journals, her last collection being *The Fault, Dear Brutus* (Keepsake Press, 1972).

ROBERT VAS DIAS was born in London in 1931 and raised and educated in the U.S.A. He has a B.A. from Grinnell College and did graduate studies at Columbia University. His publications are *Speech Acts & Happenings* (Bobbs-Merrill, 1972) and several small-press editions, the most recent of which is *Ode* (Abattoir Editions, 1977). He was the Editor for *Inside Outer Space: New Poems of the Space Age*, an anthology of contemporary American, British and Canadian poetry (Doubleday Anchor, 1970). He was Director of the National Poetry Festivals in Michigan in 1971 and 1973, and is currently Director, National Poetry Centre, and General Secretary, The Poetry Society, in London.

JOHN WAIN, poet, novelist, short-story writer, critic, biographer, autobiographer, dramatist, has published some twenty books in twenty years and is currently Professor of Poetry at Oxford University.

ANDREW WATERMAN was born in 1940 in London, and now lives in County Derry where he has been a lecturer in English since 1968 at the New University of Ulster. His first collection of poems, *Living Room* (Marvell Press, 1974), was a Poetry Book Society choice; a second volume, *From the Other Country*, published by Carcanet in 1977.

HUGO WILLIAMS was born in 1942. He has had three books of poems published by Oxford University Press – the last, *Some Sweet Day*, in 1975. He was Assistant Editor for *London Magazine* until 1970.

KIT WRIGHT was born in Kent in 1944 and from 1970 to 1975 was Education Secretary of the Poetry Society. His poems are in *Treble Poets 1* (Chatto) and *Poetry Introduction 3* (Faber). A collection, *The Bear Looked Over the Mountain* was published in 1977 by the Salamander Imprint, and he has three children's books coming out in spring 1978.